ALL ABOUT SAILING

A HANDBOOK FOR JUNIORS

MARIO BRUNET

BARRON'S EDUCATIONAL SERIES, INC.
Woodbury, N.Y. 11797

To Diane, Francine
Adèle and Jean-Louis

Cover Photo Everett Eddy
Waukegan Yacht Club, Waukegan, Illinois
(Courtesy, *Sail Magazine,* April, 1976 issue)

Written by Mario Brunet
Illustrations by René de la Haye
Photographs by Stephane Kovacs
Book design by Linda Bucholtz Ross
Translation by Andrea Rankin-Cameron

Barron's Educational Series, Inc.
113 Crossways Park Drive
Woodbury, New York 11797

ISBN 0-8120-0699-2

©Greey de Pencier Publications 1974
59 Front Street East, Toronto
Originally published in Canada

Originally published in French and
copyrighted(©) in French by Editions du Jour, 1974

PRINTED IN THE UNITED STATES OF AMERICA

CONTENTS

SAILBOATS & KIDS

To the kids

If you thought it was easy to learn to ride a two-wheeled bike you'll find it even easier to learn to sail. And while you can't very easily build your own bicycle, you can build your own sailboat!

If you run, skate, ski, roller skate, bicycle or even walk, most of your power has to come from your muscles — but when you are sailing most of it comes from the wind. It's like going down-hill all the way! Your sailboat doesn't make noise or cause pollution. It doesn't need oil or gas or even costly maintenance or repairs. All you need is a breeze— "light" for a lazy drift across rippling water or "moderate" for a fast and thrilling ride.

This book has been written just for you to help you discover how to "drive" or "sail" your boat. It is based on the Optimist sailboat — one of the least expensive yet best sailing dinghies you can find. The Optimist is sturdy, safe, lively and unsinkable. And because it is an Interna-

tional Class boat of the International Yacht Racing Union, if you have a KC number on its sail and a boat plaque you can sail your Optimist to become a world champion racer if you're seven to 15 years old.

So read on and read carefully. Look closely at the pictures. Get

some help from an adult or an older sailing friend if something seems difficult to understand. The more you learn about how to sail your boat the better your dinghy will carry you over the water and safely home again.

First read the instructions about how to use this book, then turn to Chapter One to discover all the fascinating things Mario Brunet has to say to you. Good luck and good sailing!

Howard Mountain
Parent, teacher, sailor, sailing advisor of
the Canadian Yachting Association and
friend of kids.

...& BIG PEOPLE

To the adults

All About Sailing is a primer for junior sailors ages seven to 15 using as a training dinghy the "Optimist", a safe, inexpensive, little boat you can either build or buy. This dinghy provides an excellent way to learn to sail, just for fun — or even to race at local, regional, national or international levels. Sailing the Optimist is a good way to start a lifetime interest for big and small alike.

Sailing is a sport which offers intense challenge and individual freedom. Very few sports are so relaxing and yet demand so much concentration and individual responsibility.

Although Mario Brunet has written this book for kids learning to sail, he has included special sections for you to help you with the organization, direction, supervision, testing, and safety of junior sailing participation. So if you're a seasoned sailor — or even if the only sailboats you have known have all floated in the bathtub — read this book carefully.

For more help, write to the United States Optimist-Dinghy Association, inquire at your local yacht club or sailing club, or write your regional sailing association.

Our thanks...

Barron's Educational Series, Inc., wishes to acknowledge with gratitude the assistance provided by Jim Miller, owner of the Oyster Bay Boat Shop, Oyster Bay, New York, and former Thistle national champion. Mr. Miller has been involved with junior sailing for many years and his suggestions and comments have been very helpful in preparing this volume. We wish also to thank Mr. John A. Weber of **Sailors' Gazette** for providing us with information and drawings for many of the different types of sailing dinghies described in **All About Sailing**.

READ THIS FIRST

Anyone can sail – it's easy. And this manual will tell you all you need to know to get started. There's advice on these pages about how to sail and how to sail better. There's also interesting information on wind and weather, the construction and care of small boats, games to play, knots, fitness for sailing, simple projects to make and many other things. There's even a Ship's Log where you can record the number of hours you have sailed, and keep track of your performance in regattas.

You don't need to own a dinghy to be interested in sailing and navigation. You could borrow a boat or rent one. You could even build your own boat. It's not too difficult with the help of an adult, and really not costly at all. Otherwise you may be able to use the boats at a summer camp or you may write to the yacht club nearest you about the courses offered for young people.

To make it as easy as possible for you to learn to sail, we've arranged each of the how-to-sail chapters in this book in the following way:
- first we show you what to do;
- then we send you out on the water to practice;
- next, when you're back on shore, we give you some diagrams and pictures to study, and a few tips about sailing. These are indicated with a ✪
- then, at the end of each chapter, there are some interesting games to play and puzzles and activities to do that will help you to understand it all.

The first four chapters in this book are about how to sail. You should work through them one at a time — but don't worry if some things don't seem clear. By the time you've completed Chapter Four you'll have learned enough to be racing along the water with the best of them — and safely too.

The middle part of this book is all about weather, looking after your boat, doing some projects and more. You can read these chapters in any order and you'll even find in them some things to do on a snowy winter's day in preparation for that great summer's day when you'll be out on the water again.

If you have an Optimist sailing dinghy, this book is especially for you. But even if you have another kind of boat — or no boat at all — there are many things, both informational and fun, for you on these pages. The principles of sailing are the same for all boats. With a little help from a grown-up it should be easy to adapt instruction here so that you can learn to sail any small boat with confidence.

Throughout this book you will find that we've asked you to put an "X on this boat or that boat" or "fill in some blanks". If this book is your own, go ahead and write on the pages — use it as a workbook. That's what it's meant to be. However, if the book is borrowed from a library or even a sailor friend, do your markings on a separate piece of paper. Then the next reader can have the same enjoyment from the book as you had.

Important Note: At the end of the book is a section for parents or teachers, any older person, in fact. This section includes the answers to the questions you'll be asked throughout the book and tells adults how best to help you learn about sailing. Older people needn't know how to sail to give you assistance but *they should read their chapter before you head out onto the water*. So do your very best to see that they do!

Some boats for you

You can learn to sail aboard any sort of sail-powered craft. A number of boats, however, have proven to be ideal for kids. A few of these are shown here.

We begin, first, with the Optimist dinghy because we feel that it's one of the very best boats for children. That's also why the Optimist is featured throughout this book.

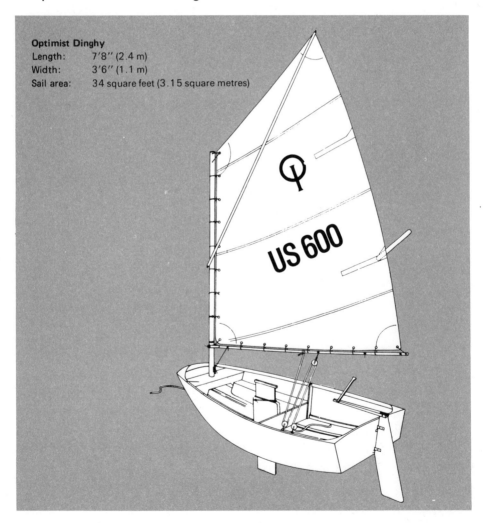

Optimist Dinghy
Length: 7′8″ (2.4 m)
Width: 3′6″ (1.1 m)
Sail area: 34 square feet (3.15 square metres)

Sabot Pram
Length: 7'8''   (2.35 m)
Width: 5'8''   (1.725 m)
Sail area: 48 square feet (4.5 square metres)

Widgeon
Length: 12'4''   (3.76 m)
Width: 5'   (1.52 m)
Sail area: 90 square feet (8.4 square metres)

Laser M
Length: 13'11''   (4.23 m)
Width: 4'6''   (1.37 m)
Sail area: 62 square feet (5.76 square metres)

Flying Junior
Length: 13'3''   (4.1 m)
Width: 4'11''   (1.5 m)
Sail area: 100 square feet (9.3 square metres)

CHAPTER 1
Learning some basics

1. Don't worry about learning a whole lot before your first outing on the water. If you head out on a fairly calm day, you'll be able to discover quite a bit about sailing by yourself.

2. Ask a parent, an instructor or an older person to help you. They should read the section for them in the back of the book and then check your answers to the questions on the following pages. They should also be responsible for your safety while you are on the water. Ask them to keep an eye on you while you are in your boat but not to shout advice. You learn by *doing* and probably won't even need their help once you are underway.

Your parents or instructors should help you anchor two buoys in the water in such a way that you can sail a practice course. (The course should be set up so you will be able to sail across the wind. Tell them to look at page 22).

3. Before setting sail do exercises 1, 2 and 3 on the following pages and have someone go over your answers. Now you're ready for Exercise 4 which involves readying your boat or "rigging it" for sailing. Have someone check to see that you've done this correctly before you leave shore.

4. Before going near the water always put on your life jacket and keep it on until the practice session is finished.

EXERCISE 1:
Thinking about sailing

If you look carefully at the drawing below you will find ten things
that *must be done* before setting
sail, and 14 things that *must
never be done*. Write "R" in the
circle beside the ten things you
think are right, and "W" beside
the 14 things you think are wrong.

Ask a parent or instructor to
check what you've done. The
answers (as are all the answers
in this book) are in the adult's
section which starts on page 161.

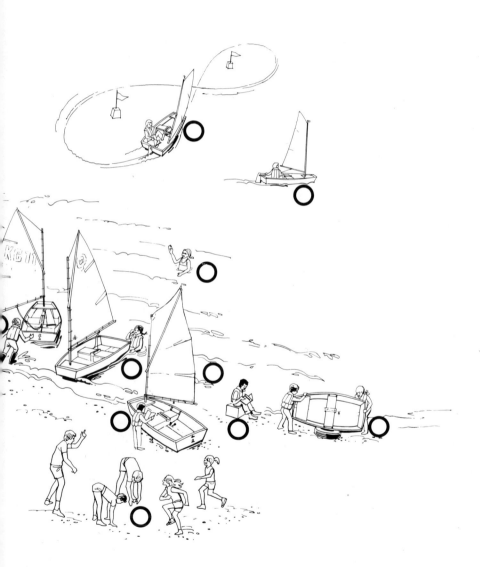

EXERCISE 2:
Planning ahead

A bird overhead gets a complete view of the shore and the water. It's useful to have such an overview of the water on which you will sail.

Look carefully at the drawings on these two pages. The first drawing shows a bird's-eye view of a lake and the second shows things that are happening on the lake. In the third drawing there are arrows which show the direction the wind is blowing. The fourth is a close up of a practice sailing course around two buoys.

Draw a bird's-eye picture of the area where you will sail. Make it large enough so that you can include: what you see (a beach, dock, cottages, flags, etc.); so that you can draw arrows indicating the direction of the wind (check to see which way it's blowing first); and so that you can draw your two buoys and sketch in a practice course for yourself similar to the one in illustration 4.

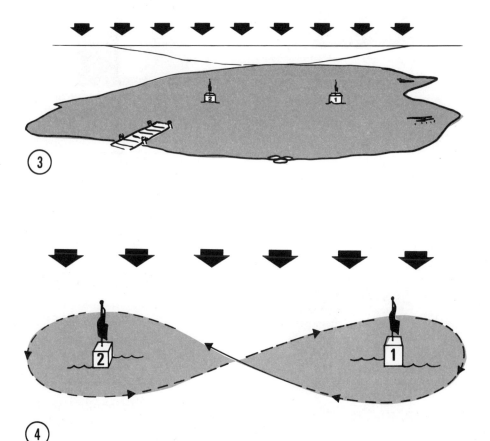

EXERCISE 3:
Some parts of your boat

The *boom* goes "boom" when it hits you on the head.

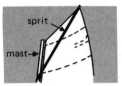

The *mast* is the pole which supports the sail. The *sprit* keeps the sail high in the air and can be adjusted to regulate the fullness of the sail.

The *tiller* is the handle or stick attached to the rudder. You use it to steer the boat.
The *rudder* cuts through the water and guides the boat; it's like a "rider" on the back of the boat.

The *daggerboard* goes down through the bottom of the boat like a dagger.

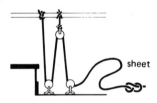
sheet

A *block* is a pulley that is used to increase a sailor's pulling power. In most small boats the sheet passes through one, two or three blocks. The *sheet* is the rope used to pull in or let out the sail.

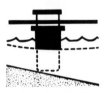

The *daggerboard trunk* holds the daggerboard; think of putting things in a trunk.

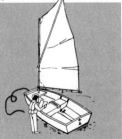

The *painter* is the rope that is tied to the front of the boat.

Look at the parts labelled on the boat opposite, then find them on your boat.

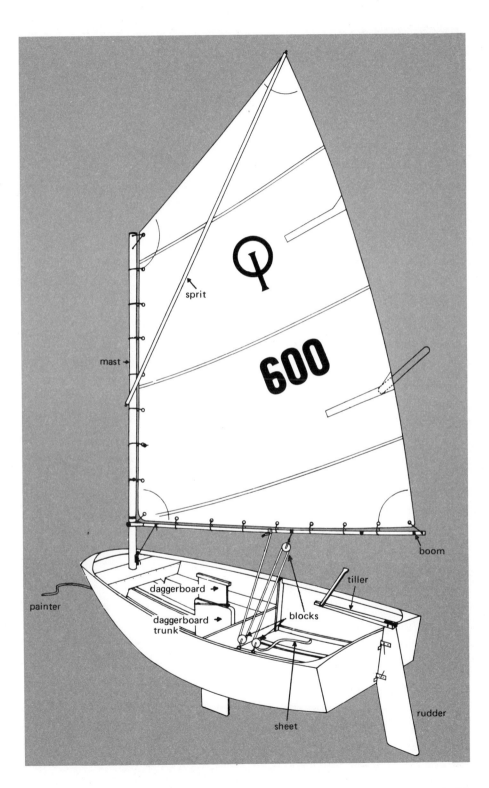

sprit

mast

600

boom

daggerboard

tiller

painter

daggerboard
trunk

blocks

sheet

rudder

EXERCISE 4:
Rigging your boat and setting sail

Until you've had some practice, you'll need assistance from a parent or instructor in rigging your boat and getting underway. Their instructions are on page 170. Follow the steps listed here and get an adult to supervise, to make sure that all the parts of your boat are properly assembled.

You can either set sail from shore or from a dock. For now you'll learn how to sail from shore. Ask an adult to make sure that your shoreline is suitable. If it isn't, follow the instructions for taking off from a dock on page 106.

1. Place the front of your boat so that it faces into the wind.
2. Find the mast, boom and sail.
3. Put the mast (with the boom and sail attached) in place.
4. Unfurl the sail so that it is free to flap in the wind.
5. Feed the rope (or "sheet" as it's called) that's attached to the boom through the blocks and tie the end of the sheet into a knot (the best kind, a Figure 8 knot, is illustrated on page 35).
6. Place the daggerboard on the floor of the boat. Also put a paddle and pail in your boat. Tie the pail to something with a rope. Check to see that there is a painter on the front of your boat.
7. Push the boat into the water and ask a friend to hold the front of the boat so it points *into the wind* while you put the rudder and tiller in position. Make sure the water is deep enough so that the rudder doesn't hit bottom.
8. Climb into the boat from the back.
9. Ask your friend to push the boat gently offshore while you insert the daggerboard in its trunk.
10. With one hand on the tiller and one hand on the sheet, sail a course similar to the one that you drew in Exercise 2.

Happy sailing! Make sure you have read the tip on page 24 (about coming back to shore) before you depart. When you return, you can study and do the rest of the tips and exercises in this chapter.

Practice on the water

Since a parent or instructor has placed two buoys as shown in the diagram here, all you have to do is to sail from one to the other — from buoy 1 to 2 and back again. Try to pass as close to the buoys as you can. You could also ask a parent or instructor to help you play some of the games described on page 171.

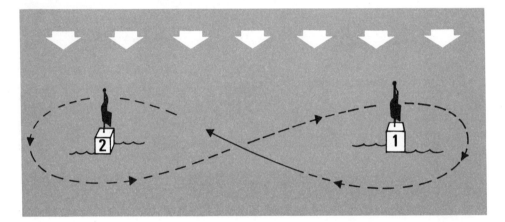

When you have completed this practice session, you can go on to study the sailing tips which follow and complete the rest of the exercises in this chapter. Don't worry if you are not able to understand the tips right away or if you are unable to complete the exercises. Try another few practice sessions on the water, sailing your boat across the wind. Also rig your boat a few more times so that this becomes easy.

✪ Coming back to shore

1. Aim at the shore. Let go of the sheet (which will stop your boat).

2. Lift out the daggerboard and place it on the bottom of your boat.

3. To avoid damaging your rudder as you sail into shallow water (that is water less than about one metre deep), jump into the water and remove the rudder before it hits bottom.

4. Let your sheet run free so that the sail can flap (or luff as it's called) and pull your boat onto the shore avoiding the rocks. Keep its nose pointed into the wind and make sure you leave your boat some distance from the water.

Lifting out the daggerboard

✪ Where to sit

On the bottom of the boat for the time being.

    You won't fall out if you are there, you'll be able to see where you are going by looking under the sail, and the boom won't hit you on the head. You'll learn more about where to sit for different conditions and manoeuvres later.

How to trim the sail

You hold the tiller with one hand and use the other to hold the sheet. Your grip on the sheet should be firm but relaxed so that you can pull the sheet to bring the sail towards you and let it run through your fingers to let the sail out.

When you pull the sail towards you, you are *sheeting in*. When you let the sail out this is called *easing the sheet*.

Ease the sheet, that is let it out, until the sail begins to luff (flutter). Then sheet in just until it stops luffing. You should watch the sail while you sheet in so that you can see when it stops luffing. Adjusting or trimming your sail this way makes your boat move quickly in the direction you are going.

The wind

The wind is a large air current which sweeps a wide area. You can see which way the wind is coming from by looking at a flag, smoke, trees, or ripples on the water. Waves often move in the same direction as the wind but may not — as the direction of the wind changes faster than the direction of the waves.

When your boat is not moving, your wind indicator on your mast shows the true direction from which the wind is coming. A north wind blows from the north, an east wind blows from the east . . . and so on.

We can show the direction of the wind on a drawing or photograph by drawing several arrows which point *in the direction the wind is going* (see opposite).

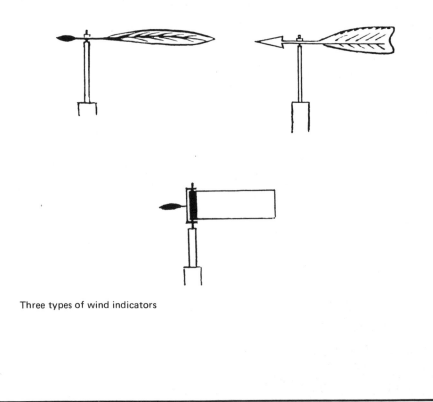

Three types of wind indicators

Sailing on a beam reach

Sailing across the wind is called sailing on a beam reach. The wind comes across the side of the boat.

Bow and stern

The front or the nose of the boat is the bow of the boat.
The back of the boat is the stern.

Making the most of the wind

For a boat to move ahead, the sail must be billowed out, or full of wind. You can fill your sail (or make it pull well) by changing the direction of the boat with the tiller, by adjusting the sail with the sheet (either by sheeting in or by easing the sheet) or both. It's fun to experiment on the water to find out what makes your boat sail best – and fastest.

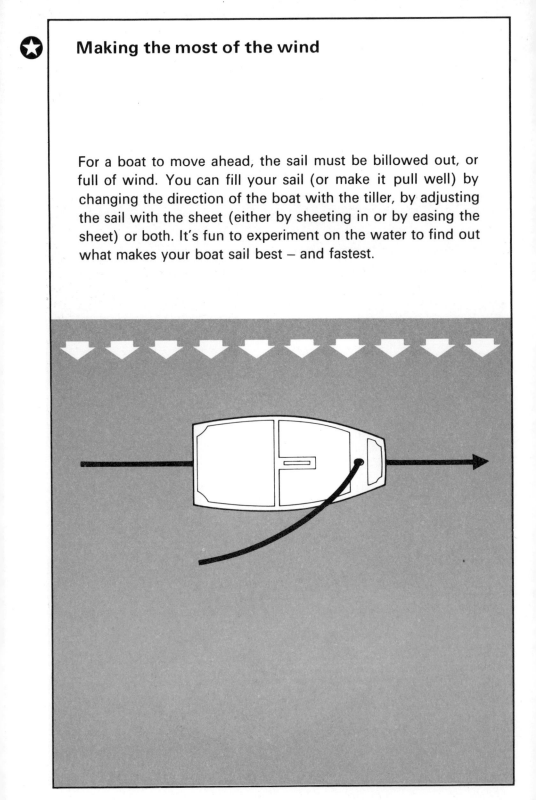

Being "in irons"

When the front of your boat is pointed straight in the direction from which the wind is coming and your sheet is completely loose, your sail will flap like a flag. You won't move ahead and you may move backwards. This is called being "in irons".

To get out of irons and get going again, hold the boom out to one side of the boat and push the tiller to the same side. When the boat begins to turn, sheet in and move the tiller to steer the course you want.

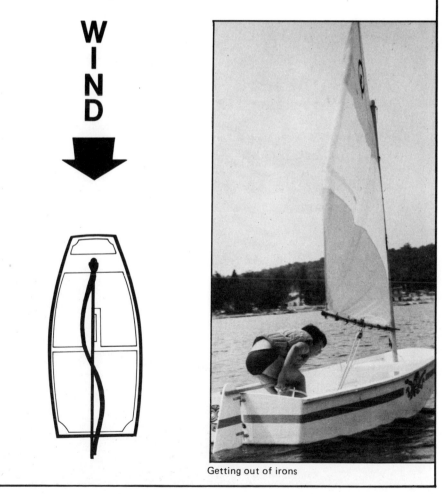

Getting out of irons

Dinghy capacity

This small craft with one sail is designed to be sailed by *one* person. But it can be sailed by two people – either two children or an adult and a child.

Figure 8 knot

This knot is easy to tie. It is a stopper knot and prevents the sheet from running through the block. It is tied at the end of the sheet.

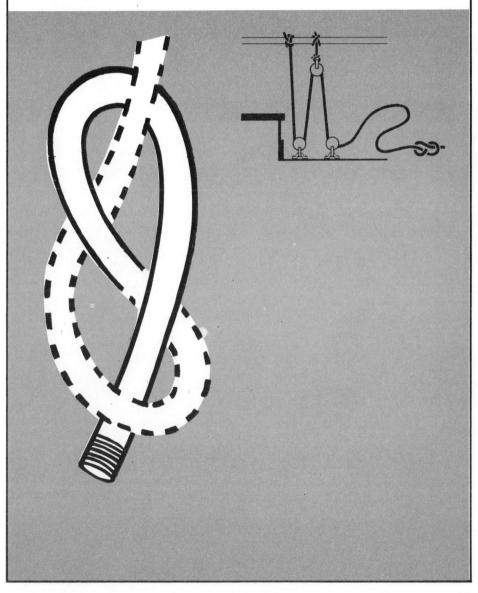

Clove hitch

The clove hitch is a very old sailor's knot. It is used today because it is simple, practical and efficient (like all marine knots). You can use it, for example, to tie your painter to a post.

The step-by-step diagrams on this page will teach you how to tie the knot. The secret is practice.

You should be able to tie this knot quickly with your eyes closed. Practice on a broom handle. Don't pull too much on your rope after you've tied the knot because this very strong knot can be hard to undo when it's tied tightly.

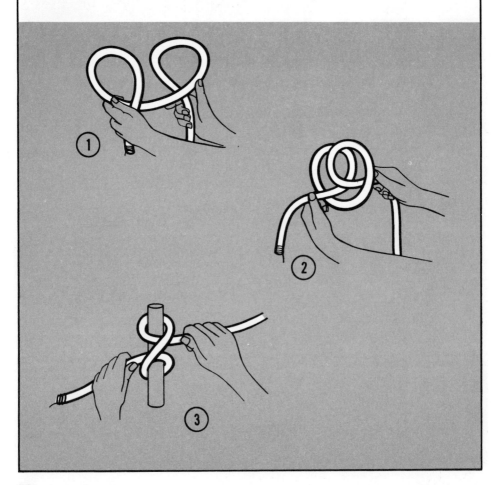

★ Stopping your boat

There is no real way to "put on your brakes" in a sailboat. If you want to stop — or at least slow down in a hurry — for some reason, ease the sheet until the sail flutters or "luffs". Or point your bow up into the wind. Always remember that a boat that is not moving cannot be steered.

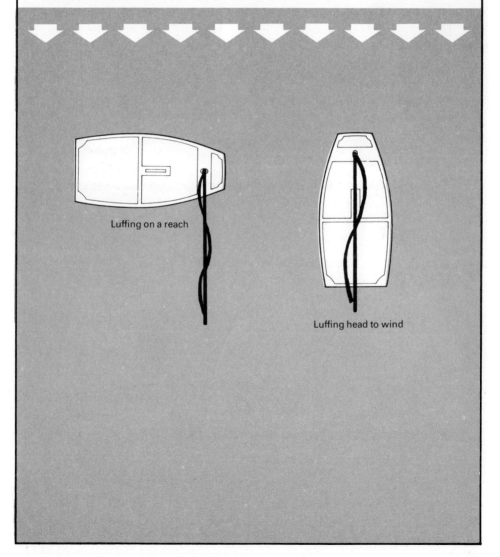

Luffing on a reach

Luffing head to wind

EXERCISE 5:
The heel of your boat

Sailing dinghies under most conditions are meant to be sailed flat on the water. Put a cross (X) beside the boats that seem to be flattest on the water.

EXERCISE 6:
How to hold the sheet

Put a cross (X) beside the drawing which shows how to hold the sheet correctly.

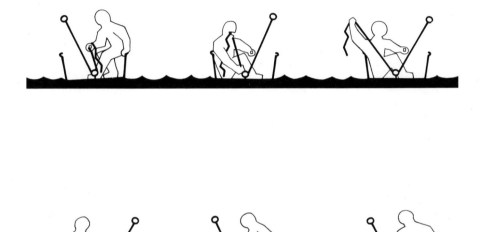

EXERCISE 7:
Identifying other boats

Most small boats have a sign or an insignia on the sail which identifies them. Here are a few. See how many you can spot on the water.

Sunfish	Force 5	International 470	Thistle
Optimist International	Albacore	Butterfly	OK Dinghy
Snipe	Fireball	International 420	Flying Scot
Laser	Lightning	Hobie Cat 14	Flying Junior

EXERCISE 8:
Wind direction

Check off the objects in the following list which could indicate the direction of the wind.

_____ tree without leaves
_____ tree with leaves
_____ flag
_____ roof
_____ car
_____ hair
_____ smoke
_____ clouds
_____ waves
_____ weather vane
_____ wet finger

EXERCISE 9:
Quiz

1. What do the following words make you think of? Boom, daggerboard, daggerboard trunk, rudder.

2. Where should you sit in the boat?

3. Should you use only one hand to tighten the sheet (pull it towards you)?

4. If your sail is "luffing" will your boat go faster or slower?

5. What must you do to get the wind to fill your sail?

6. Name four things that you must do when you are taking your boat into the shore.

7. How do you indicate the direction of the wind on a drawing?

8. Draw a boat sailing on a beam reach.

9. Draw a boat. Circle the bow and draw a square around the stern.

10. Draw a boat facing into the wind, "in irons".

CHAPTER 2
Getting some practice

1. When you have done the first course (sailing on a beam reach) on the water several times you are ready to begin Chapter 2. Now is the time to ask your instructors any questions that puzzle you.

2. Ask a parent or instructor to participate; they can check your answers and be responsible for your safety while you are on the water. One of the first things they can do is to place three buoys on the water in the same relation to the wind as shown on page 46 so that you can complete the practice course.

3. Make sure you have done the exercise on page 41, then do the three exercises on page 45.

4. Look again at the sailing tip on page 28 and remember to ask yourself from time to time while you are on the water "where is the wind coming from?"

5. Look at pages 46 and 47, Practice on the Water.

6. Before doing anything, put on your life jacket and keep it on until the practice session is finished.

7. You are now ready to rig your boat, following the steps outlined on pages 20 and 21.

EXERCISE 10:
Thinking about sailing

The drawing in Exercise 1 on pages 14 and 15 represents ten things that must be done before setting sail, and 14 things that must never be done. *Write down the ten correct actions in the spaces below.*

_____   _____
_____   _____
_____   _____
_____   _____
_____   _____

EXERCISE 11:
Planning ahead

Draw a bird's-eye view of the water for this practice session as you did in Exercise 2 on pages 16 and 17. Remember you are now drawing the course you will follow to complete Chapter 2 – (read the instructions for the practice session on the water on the next page). You should also indicate on your drawing the position of your boat and of your sail between buoys 1 and 2.

EXERCISE 12:
Rigging your boat and setting sail

Follow the steps outlined in Exercise 4 on pages 20 and 21.

Practice on the water

Since a parent or instructor has placed three buoys as in the diagram below you have only to sail from one to the other— from 1 to 2 to 3. Keep to the right of each buoy, and try to pass as close to each one as possible without touching it.

Your parents or instructors could also help you play some of the games described on page 171.

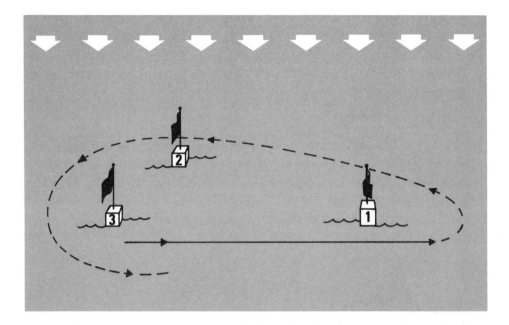

Don't worry if you are not able to understand right away the sailing tips which follow or if you are unable to complete the follow-up exercises. Try the first practice session on the water and this one several more times. What is important is that you are able to sail your boat according to the bird's-eye view of the course you drew in Exercise 11 on the previous page.

Note: Study the following tips and do the exercises only after you have been on the water.

47

Left and right sides of the boat

In order to determine which is the right side and which is the left side of a boat you must look towards the bow. From this position the boat is divided down the middle into right and left sides.

Port and starboard

The proper nautical term for the left side of the boat is port; for the right side of the boat is starboard. Here's how to remember which is which: "left" has four letters and so does "port". If you remember this, then you will know that the right side of the boat must be starboard.

When boats are travelling in the dark, they carry running lights to indicate their position and direction to others. The light on the port side of a boat is red, on the starboard side, green. You can see these lights from shore – because, of course, you won't be sailing your small boat at night!

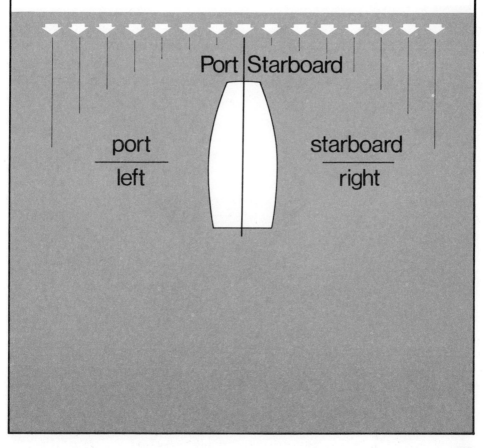

Sailing close hauled

Sailing with the wind blowing in the direction shown in the diagram is called sailing *close hauled* or *beating* into the wind. Most boats are unable to sail any closer to the direction from which the wind is coming than those in the diagram. If you sail any closer to the wind your boat will not make good progress. Sailing too close to the wind is called *pinching*.

When you are sailing close hauled your sail should be pulled in to the edge of your stern (see the diagram below). Steer your boat until the sail just stops luffing to make your boat move ahead well.

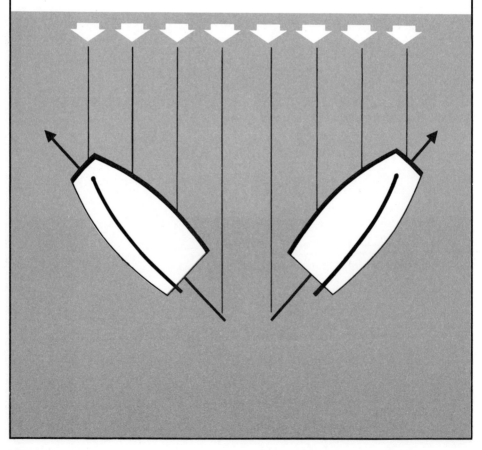

Sailing on a broad reach

This means to sail or to be pushed almost with the wind. The wind blows half on the side of the boat and half on the stern.

Your sail should be farther out (see the diagram below) to pull well. Let it out until it starts luffing, then sheet in until it is pulling well.

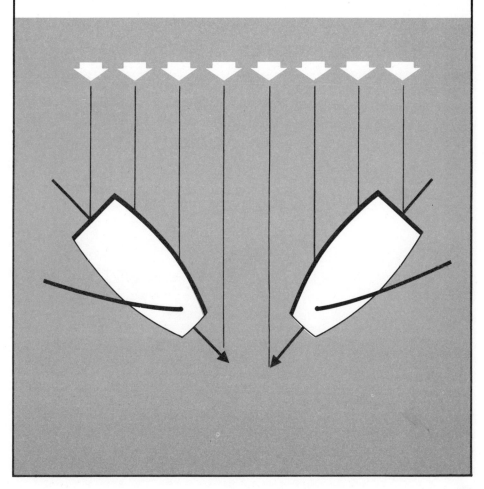

Coming about and gybing

These are two ways to change the direction of your boat, so that the wind blows on the opposite side.

A.1. Before "coming about" the wind blows on the port side

A.2. After "coming about" the wind blows on the starboard side of the boat.

B.3. Before "gybing" the wind blows on the port side of the

B.4. After "gybing" the wind blows on the starboard side of the boat.

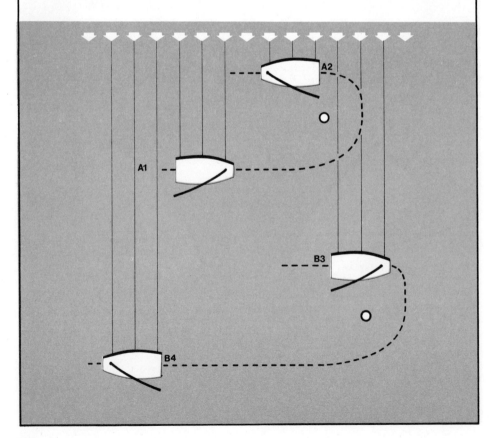

A.5. When you come about you turn your boat into the wind.
B.6. When you gybe you turn your boat away from the wind;
and the sail passes quickly from one side to the other.

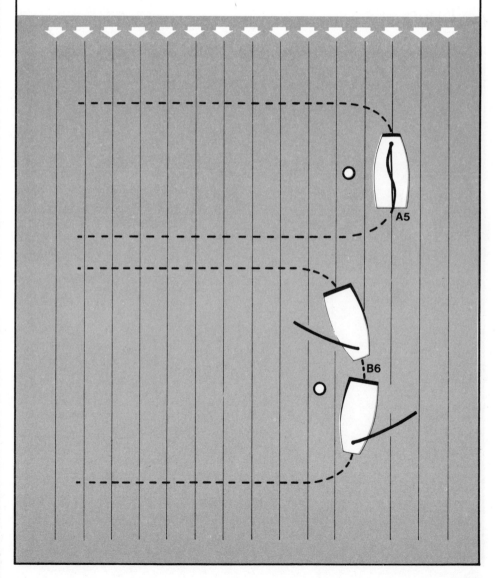

Two ways to go round a buoy

You can go around each buoy in two different ways (except in regattas): by coming about (as shown in No. 1 in the illustration below) where the boat faces into the wind, or by gybing (as in No. 2 in the illustration below). The boat moves away from the wind.

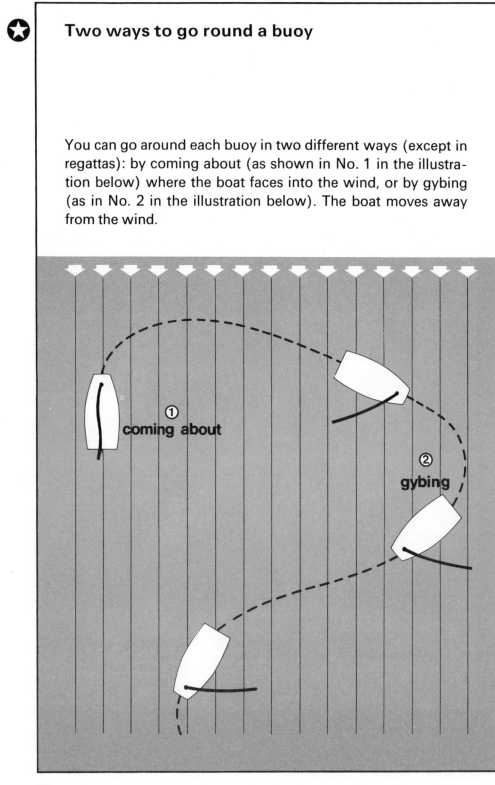

What the daggerboard does

The wheels of a car are like the daggerboard. If a boat is pushed straight ahead, the daggerboard doesn't slow down its movement, and the boat advances, just like the car in the first picture. But if the boat is pushed from the side, the dagger-board prevents it from moving, just like the wheels of the car in the second picture.

EXERCISE 13:
Port and starboard sides of your boat

Put (P) on the port sides of the boats in the diagrams below and (S) on the starboard sides.

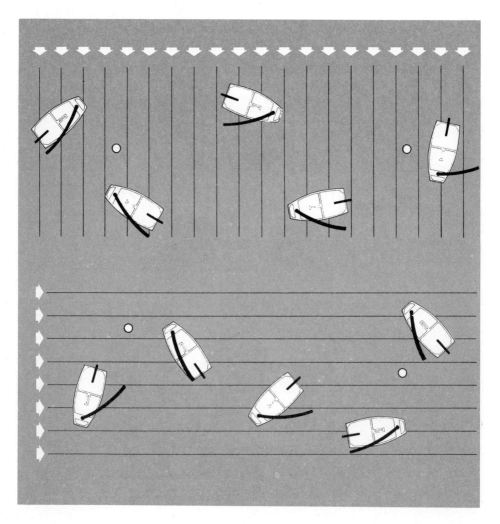

EXERCISE 14:
The action of your daggerboard

If you push the triangular piece of ice in the drawing with a pencil as shown, which way will the wedge move? Circle the correct answer, A, B, or C.

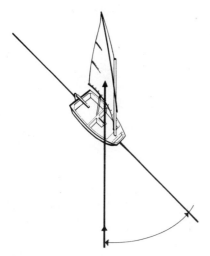

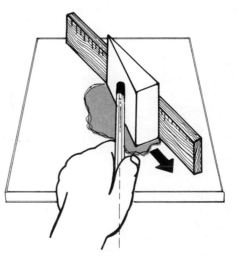

The wind pushes on the sail and the daggerboard changes the power so that the boat moves forward over the water.

The pencil pushes on the wedge and the ruler changes the power so that the ice moves forward along the table.

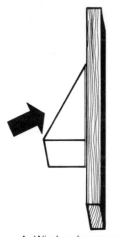

A Wind pushes on sail

B Daggerboard pushes on water

C Boat moves ahead

EXERCISE 15:
Coming about and gybing

Look at the route taken by the boat around each buoy. At each turn mark "C" if the boat had to "come about" to complete the turn, or "G" if the boat "gybed" to complete the turn.

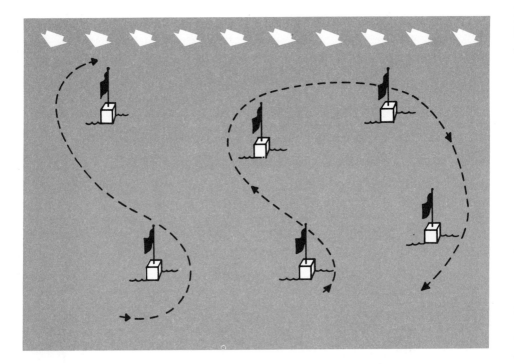

EXERCISE 16:
Positions of your sail

Draw a line on each boat to indicate the position of the sail which would make the boat move forward at its best speed. Pay attention to the direction of the wind as indicated by the arrows. Think about the positions of your sail when you were out on the water.

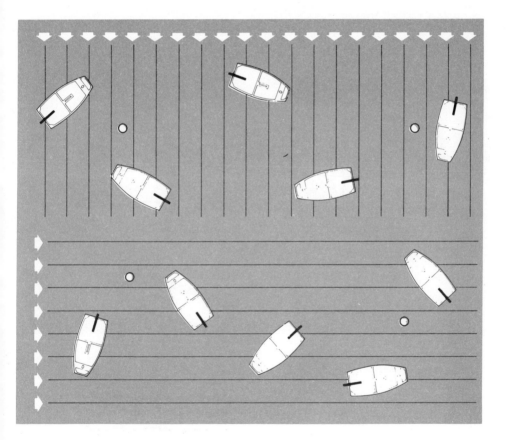

EXERCISE 17:
Analogies

The objects in column 1 come from Exercise 14 on page 57, column 2 lists part of your dinghy. Draw a line to connect each object in column 1 with the object in column 2 which has a similar function.

pencil

boat

ice wedge

wind

table

daggerboard

ruler

water

EXERCISE 18:
Quiz

1. What happened when you changed direction to go around buoys 1 and 2?

2. Draw some arrows on a piece of paper to indicate the direction of the wind, and then draw three boats in different sailing positions – the first *close hauled*, the second on a *beam reach* and third on a *broad reach*. Don't forget to indicate the bow of each boat and the position of the sail.

3. Name at least three things around you which could indicate to you the direction of the wind.

4. Give the steps for setting sail and for returning to the shore.

5. How do you determine the left and right side of a boat?

6. How many ways are there to change the direction of your boat so that the wind is blowing first on one side of the boat and then on the other? Name them.

CHAPTER 3
Becoming proficient

1. You will have to concentrate to successfully complete the manoeuvre in this chapter, Before you set sail – and throughout your practice session in the water – you must continuously ask yourself from which direction the wind is blowing.

2. Ask a parent or instructor to continue to participate; to check your answers to the questions in this chapter and be responsible for your safety while you are on the water. They should first place four buoys on the water in the same relation to the wind as shown on page 64 so that you can complete the practice course.

3. Do exercises 19, 20 and 21. Look once again at the sailing tips on page 50 and 51.

4. Before doing anything, put on your life jacket and keep it on until the practice session is finished.

5. You are now ready to rig your boat, following the procedure already learned on pages 20 and 21.

EXERCISE 19:
Thinking about sailing

Color green the correct activities in the drawing in Exercise 1 on pages 14 and 15. Color red the activities that are wrong.

EXERCISE 20:
Planning ahead

Draw a bird's-eye view of the water for this practice session as you did in Exercise 2 on pages 16 and 17. Remember that you are now drawing the course you will follow to complete Chapter 3 (read the instructions for the practice session on the water on the next pages). You should also indicate on your drawing the position of your boat and of your sail between buoys 1 and 2, 2 and 3, 3 and 4, 4 and 1.

EXERCISE 21:
Rigging your boat and setting sail

Describe to your instructor, as if you were actually doing it, how you rig your boat and leave the shore.

Practice on the water

Since a parent or instructor has placed four buoys as in the diagram below you have only to sail from one buoy to the other — from 1 to 2 to 3 to 4. Try to pass as close as possible to each buoy. Once you have gone around number 4 you should come back to number 1.

Your parents or instructors could also help you play the games described on page 171.

When you have completed your practice session on the water and have studied the sailing tips which follow, try to complete the follow-up exercises at the end of the chapter.

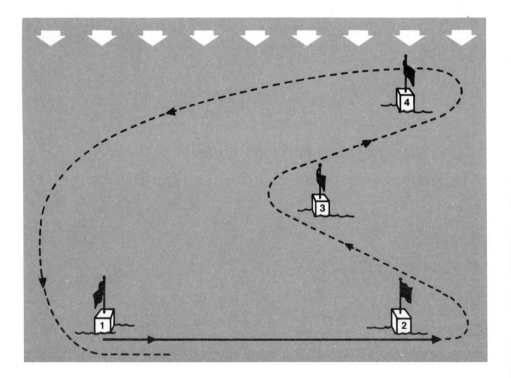

Note: Study the following sailing tips and do the exercises only after you have been on the water.

To be windward or leeward

The wall in the first diagram protects the boy from the wind. His flag does not flutter because it does not receive any wind. It's the wall which receives the wind first. The boy is in the lee of the wall or *leeward* (pronounced loo-ward) of the wall.

The boy in the second diagram receives the wind before the wall does. His flag flutters. He is *windward* of the wall.

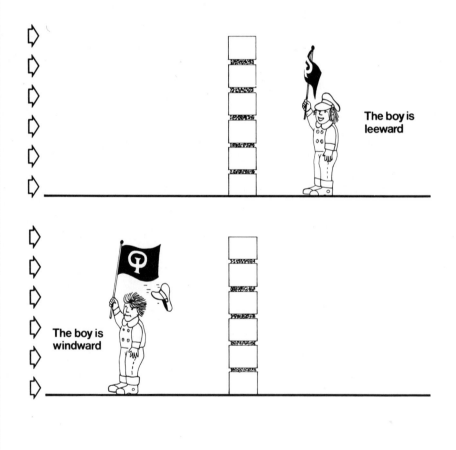

The boy is leeward

The boy is windward

Leeward and windward sides of your boat

The *leeward* side of your boat is the side furthest away from the direction from which the wind is coming. Generally, your sail when filled with wind is on the leeward side of your boat.

The *windward* side of your boat is the side which receives the wind first. This is generally the side opposite the sail.

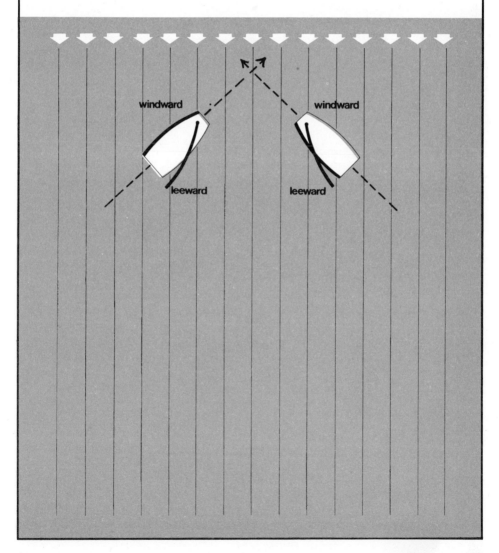

Sailing to windward

Sailing to windward means to be beating or sailing close hauled at an angle to the wind. To sail from buoy 1 to buoy 4 in the diagram below, you have to sail your boat so that the wind first blows on one side of the sail and then on the other.

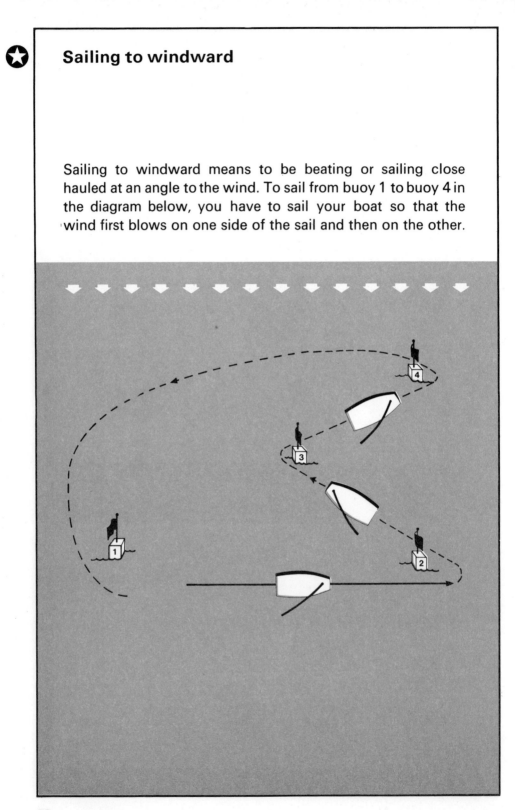

Running with the wind

Running with the wind means to sail in the same direction as the wind. The wind blows straight on the stern of your boat. The boat gybes to get around buoy number 1.

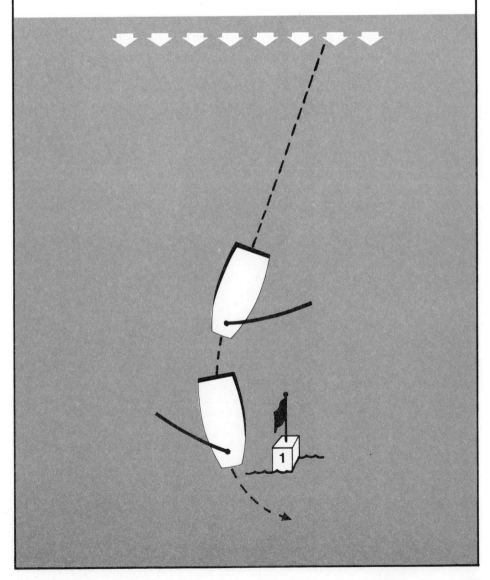

Tacks

Since the wind can come across either the port or the star-board side of a boat, there are two tacks – a port tack and a starboard tack. *Tack* is the word used to describe the side of the boat which receives the wind first.

When a boat is on a port tack the wind blows across the port side (i.e. the port side is windward). When a boat is on a starboard tack the wind blows across the starboard side (i.e. the starboard side is windward).

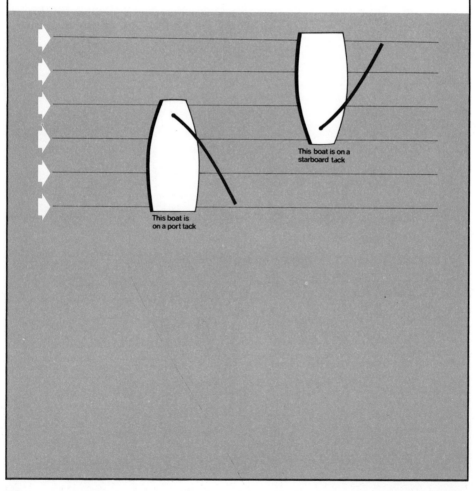

This boat is on a
starboard tack

This boat is
on a port tack

The best way to come about

To make your boat come about efficiently you should:

1. Sail close to the wind.

2. If necessary, veer away from the wind just a little to pick up some speed.

3. Push the tiller to the leeward side of the boat – the boat will turn and the sail will swing across to the other side. You change position so that you face the sail again, and change hands on the tiller and sheet.

4. Adjust your tiller so that you are sailing on your new tack.

Remember, if you have crew aboard, shout "Ready About" before you come about – so that they'll be prepared. Then shout "Hard Alee" as you push the tiller, so they'll know to duck under the boom!

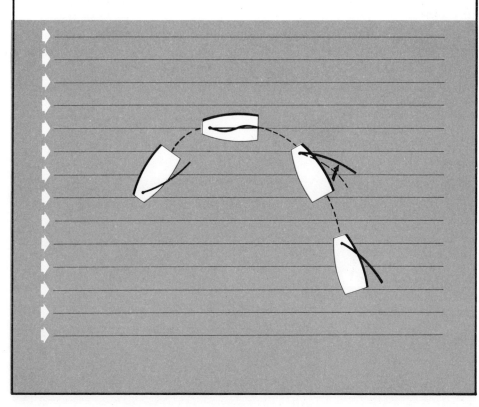

The best way to gybe

You can gybe without changing the direction of your boat. The sail passes from the right side (see 1 below) to the left side (see 2 below) while the boat goes in the same direction. There is no turn but there is still a *gybe*. All that changes is the tack. First the boat is on a starboard tack (the sail is on the left side of the boat, even though the wind is coming from behind), then on a port tack (the sail moved over to the right side).

Another way to gybe a small boat is to:

1. Pull your daggerboard up (but not so high as it gets in the way of the boom).
2. Sheet in a little so that your sail is trimmed a little closer than it was when you were running.
3. Pull your tiller away from the boom. Duck! The sail and boom will swing quickly over to the other side of your boat.
4. If you have crew aboard, warn them you are about to gybe by shouting "Gybe Ho". As you pull the tiller over, shout "Boom Over", so your crew will know when to duck.
5. After the boom has swung over, move quickly to the other side of your boat.
6. Straighten your tiller and . . .
7. Ease your sheet so that your sail is set for running again.

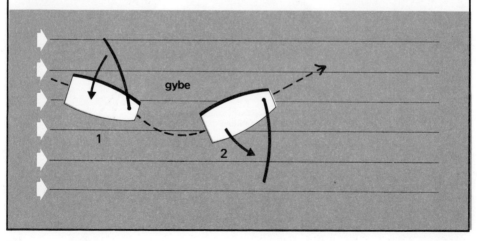

gybe

1

2

Points of sail

A point of sail is the term given to the position of the bow of your boat in relation to the direction of the wind. Here are four points of sail.

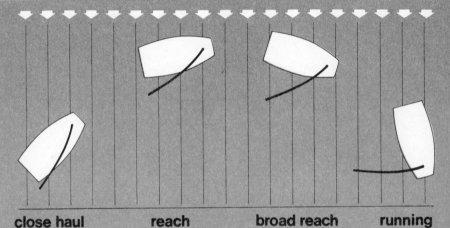

| close haul or beat | reach | broad reach | running |

The points of sail for each tack

There is a port tack and a starboard tack for each point of sail: close haul, beam reach, broad reach, and running.

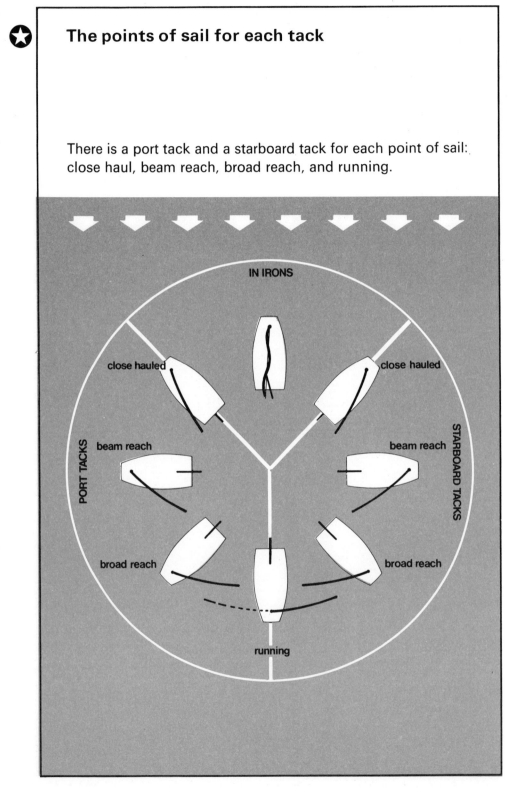

Positioning your daggerboard

Think back to the comparison between the daggerboard and the wheels of the car in the previous chapter. Your daggerboard is just like the wheels of the car. It prevents your boat from being pushed sideways.

1. The closer you sail to the direction from which the wind is coming, the more the wind tries to push your boat sideways. So, when you are beating or sailing close hauled, push your daggerboard as far down as it will go in the water. This will keep your boat moving forward instead of slipping sideways.

2. When you are on a reach you are sailing across the wind. The wind doesn't push your boat sideways as much as when you're sailing close hauled. Therefore you can pull your daggerboard part way up. Without your daggerboard dragging in the water as much as it did you'll move faster.

3. When you are on a run the wind pushes your boat ahead, so you don't need your daggerboard at all. Pull it right up (but not so high that it gets in the way of the boom) or pull it out of the daggerboard trunk and place it in the bottom of your boat.

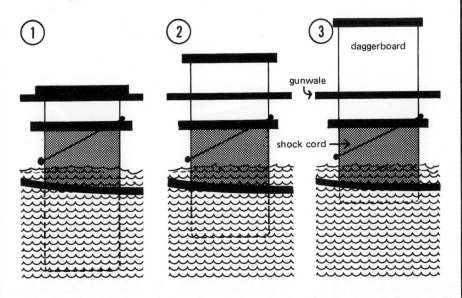

Bowline

The bowline knot if tied properly cannot slip. It also is easily untied. Because it provides a temporary loop in the end of a rope or line, it has many uses, for example attaching the line to the boom.

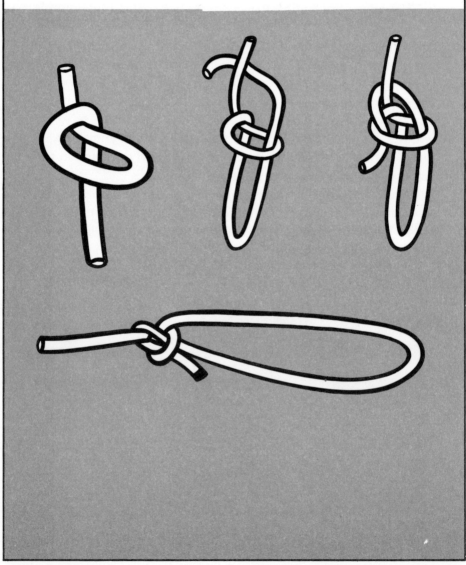

Sailing from shore when the wind is strong

Sometimes when there's a strong onshore breeze, it is difficult to get your boat underway before the wind and the waves push you back to shore. This is especially true in shallow water because you can't lower your daggerboard very far without hitting bottom.

The best way to get going is to have someone stand in the water and hold your boat until you're organized. When you are ready, have them point your bow so that you can sail away on a beam reach on the tack that gets you away from shore the fastest.

Once underway, sheet in quickly so that your sail is pulling well and your boat moves quickly. Then lower your daggerboard to the correct position.

When there's a strong onshore wind and the waves are high, come back to shore by sailing on a beam reach. Before you get to the breakers or the surf pull out your daggerboard and put it in the bottom of your boat. Remove your rudder and tiller. Keep your boat moving quickly along on a beam reach and sail right up onto the beach. As soon as you touch shore let go of your sheet and jump out of your boat. Pull your boat as fast as you can out of the water.

Reef or square knot

The reef knot is used to tie together two ropes of equal size.

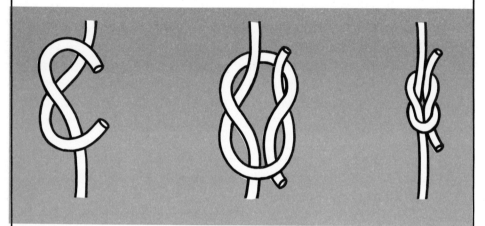

Round turn and two half hitches

This is a useful knot for tying your painter to a ring or post. If you loop your rope twice around the ring or post this knot cannot work itself loose.

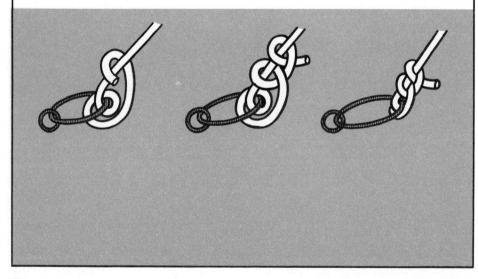

✪ Coiling

The best way of keeping lines or ropes from getting tangled is to coil them. Most sailors coil lines clockwise and loop them as shown in the diagram below.

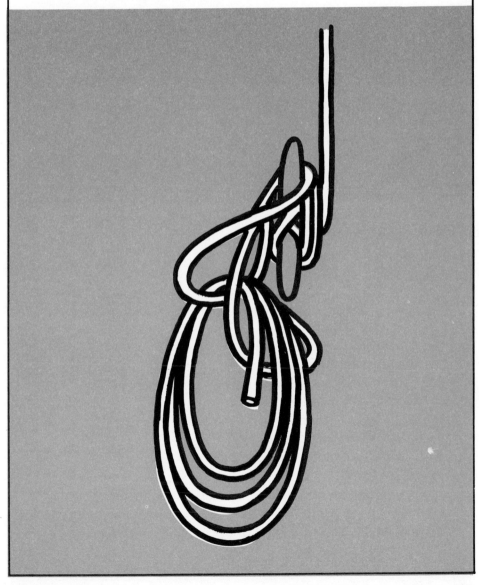

More parts of your boat

You have already learned names for a number of parts of your boat. To become a proficient sailor, however, you need to know what every part of your boat is called. Below are some names and descriptions. Locate them on the boat opposite and then find them on your own boat.

1. Transom – the piece across the stern
2. Pintels and Gudgeons—pintels and gudgeons hold your rudder on your boat. Pintels are pins that fit in the holes in the gudgeons.
3. Gunwale (pronounced gunnel) – top of the sides of your boat
4. Shock cord – holds daggerboard in place
5. Hiking straps – you hook your toes under them to keep from falling out when you hike out
6. Mast step – where the bottom of the mast rests
7. Mast thwart – support for your mast at the level of the gunwales
8. Buoyancy – every boat must have enough buoyancy material to keep it afloat when it is filled with water, and crew!
9. Cringle – eyes or holes in the sail which ropes can pass through
10. Lacing – holds the sail to the mast
11. Swivel – attaches the block to the boom
12. Luff – forward edge of sail
13. Head—top edge of sail
14. Leech – back edge of sail
15. Batten – thin slats which prevent the leech from flapping
16. Batten pocket – pockets into which battens fit
17. Foot – bottom edge of sail
18. Peak—top corner of sail
19. Clew – bottom back corner of sail
20. Tack – bottom forward corner of sail
21. Class number
22. Black bands – the marks on the mast and boom which indicate the maximum amount the sail can be pulled out.
23. Outhaul – line at the end of the boom used to put tension on the foot of the sail

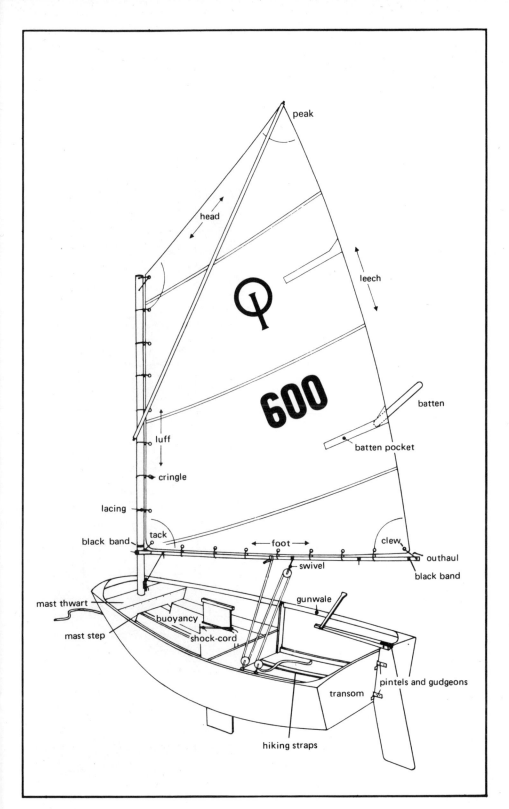

peak

head

leech

batten

batten pocket

luff

cringle

lacing

600

tack

black band

foot

clew

outhaul

black band

swivel

mast thwart

buoyancy

gunwale

mast step

shock-cord

pintels and gudgeons

transom

hiking straps

EXERCISE 22:
The points of sail

1. Can the boat in diagram A move forward?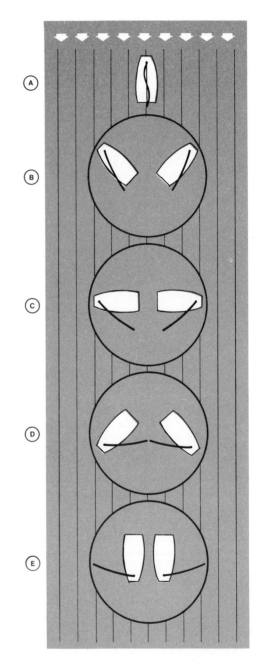

2. Are the boats in diagram B on a beat, a beam reach or a run?

3. What about the boats in diagram C, D and E?

4. Which boats in B, C, D or E will move ahead the fastest?

5. Which boats will move ahead most slowly?

EXERCISE 23:
Sails which luff and sails which pull well

Look at the three pairs of boats. In each pair one boat moves ahead and the other doesn't. What makes one boat advance?

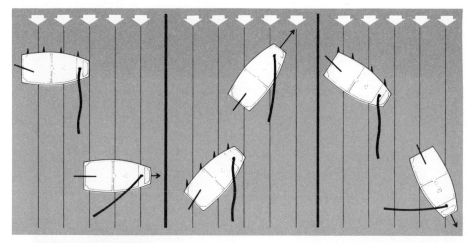

EXERCISE 24:
Action of the daggerboard

Look at the three pairs of boats. One boat of each pair has its daggerboard down, the other does not. Which boats will move forward the fastest?

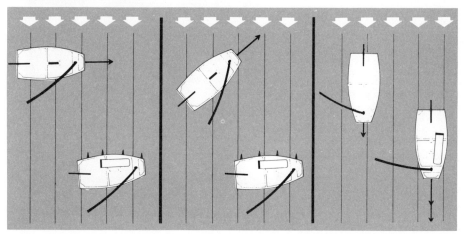

EXERCISE 25:
Windward and leeward

A. Look at the three pairs of boats. Draw a circle around the boat in each pair which is *leeward* of the other.

B. Draw a circle around anything which is to *windward* of the boat.

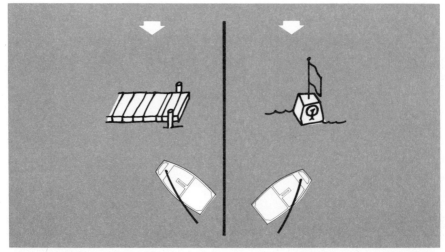

C. Mark the leeward side of the boat with an "L", mark the windward side with a "W".

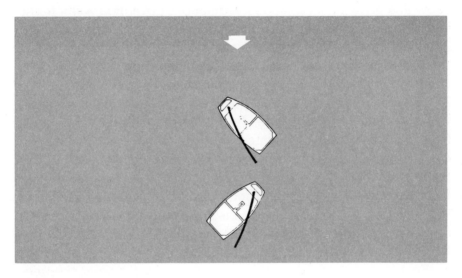

EXERCISE 26:
Quiz

1. What are two ways of stopping a boat on the water?
2. How do you remember which side is port and which side is starboard?
3. What is a point of sail?
4. What does tack mean?
5. Is there a port tack and a starboard tack for each point of sail?
6. What does "beating" mean?

CHAPTER 4

Now that you're a sailor

1. Since you are now able to sail your dinghy with some skill, this chapter will teach you how to race in regattas. You will have to know and obey the international regulations governing water traffic in order to avoid collisions and spills.

2. Ask a parent or instructor to place buoys on the water (in the same relation to the wind as shown on page 88) in such a way that you can complete the practice regatta course on the water.

3. Parents or instructors should give the starting signal and supervise the running of the regatta. They will need a loudspeaker, some flags, a whistle and a stop watch.

4. Ask your parents or instructors not to shout sailing advice. This regatta will allow you to see how you manage by yourself in your first race. (Perhaps you will discover some of the tricks permitted in the regulations to help you go faster.) You will choose your own route between buoy 1 and 2.

5. Before heading out onto the water do exercises 27, 28 and 29.

6. Reread the sailing tips and exercises in the previous chapters.

7. Before doing anything put on your life jacket and keep it on until the end of the race.

8. You are now ready to rig your boat, remembering the steps outlined on pages 20 and 21.

EXERCISE 27:
Learning the "rules of the road"

Read the sailing tips on pages 91, 92, 93 and 94.

EXERCISE 28:
Review

Re-read exercise 1 on pages 14 and 15. As a matter of habit by now you should be keeping an eye on the weather. Draw a bird's-eye view of the water as you did in exercise 2 on pages 16 and 17, and mark your regatta course on it. Draw a series of small boats on your drawing to show how your boat will sail the course. Indicate the position of the sail on each boat you draw. Read the practice session on the water, on pages 88-89. Study the course carefully to determine if there are currents or sheltered areas where there is no wind.

EXERCISE 29:
Keeping your boat ship-shape

Is your dinghy clean? Whether it be wood or fibreglass, wash it inside and out, until its hull shines. (You should do this regularly.)

How about your sail? Does it need a wash too? If so, wash it in mild soapy water and hang it out to dry. You can wash your sheet and any other ropes or lines in the same way.

Practice on the water

One of your parents or an instructor has placed the buoys as indicated below: you must cross the starting line when the signal is given (either a blast from a whistle or a wave of a flag). Then you will have to *beat* up to buoy number 2, and *run* back to buoy number 1 to come over the finish line.

It is difficult to cross the starting line exactly when the signal is given. It will probably be necessary to restart several times before you can control your boat completely.

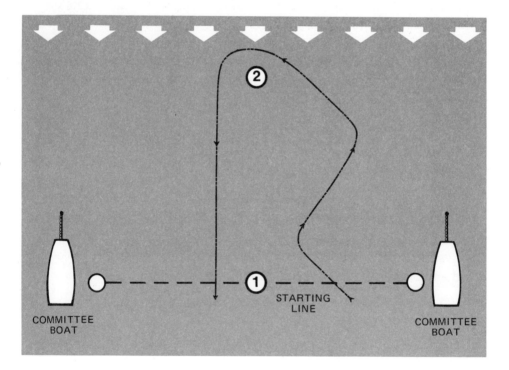

If there are a lot of competitors the course could be longer, like the ones illustrated below.

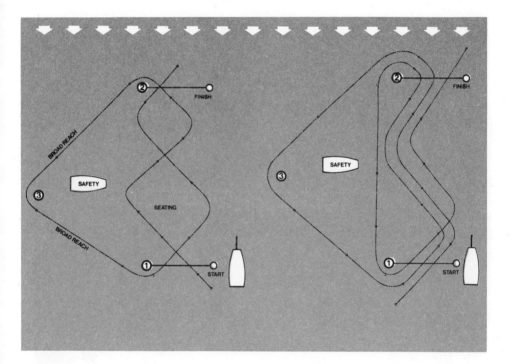

EXERCISE 30:
Equipment check

Examine the mast, boom, sprit and sail to see if everything is sound and assembled and adjusted correctly. When you are underway your sail should be smooth without wrinkles or bags.

Right of way: Rule 1

Racing rules are numerous and sometimes complicated, but to make racing fair to everyone, here and on the next few pages, are a few suggestions to get you started.
A boat on a starboard tack always has the right of way. A boat on a port tack must let a boat on a starboard tack pass.

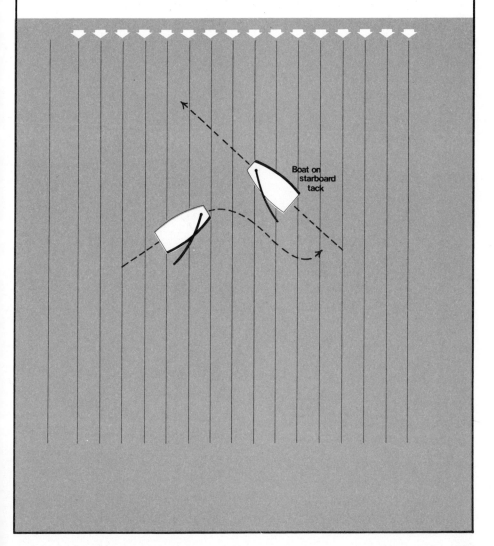

Boat on starboard tack

Right of way: Rule 2

A boat which catches up with another boat may pass to the right or left of the course the boat is sailing.

Right of way: Rule 3

Mostly the overtaking boat must avoid the boat it is passing. A boat to leeward has the right of way.

Racing buoys

You must *never touch* a racing buoy. You have to pass as close as possible to the buoys without touching them. If you touch one you will be disqualified under the International Racing Regulations unless you go round the buoy again without touching it. The Regulations determining the right of way are like the highway code. They help to prevent accidents which might injure you and damage your boat. They must be *obeyed* at all times.

Right of way: Rule 4

Buoy room! When the helmsman (the one who is holding the tiller) of one boat shouts, "Buoy room!", the other boat must move out of the way to give him room to manoeuvre.

In the drawing below, the outside boat "B" must leave the inside boat "P" enough room to go around the buoy.

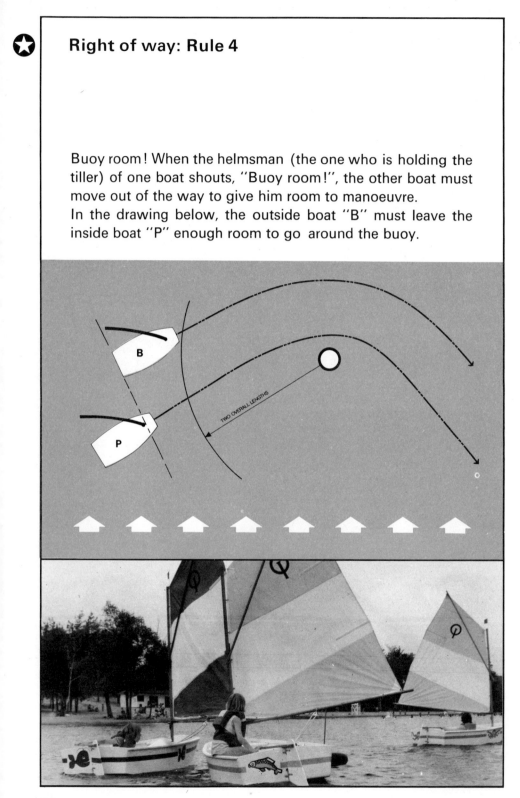

Sailing to windward

You can walk straight up a steep mountain but you can't sail straight up the wind. When you want to walk up a mountain, the easiest way is to climb a zig-zag path. When you want to sail in the direction from which the wind is coming, you first sail close hauled on one tack and then on the other. Because you change back and forth from one tack to another this zig-zagging is called tacking.

Sailing downwind

You can come down a mountain without zig-zagging. In a boat you can sail downwind without zig-zagging. But just as you have to step carefully coming down a hill, you have to sail carefully downwind. You don't want to gybe or change from one tack to another by accident. If you gybe accidentally in heavy winds the bow of your boat may dig into the water and the boat may turn right into the wind (this is called broaching) and perhaps capsize. If it starts to roll back and forth, trim the sail in. (see figure 3).

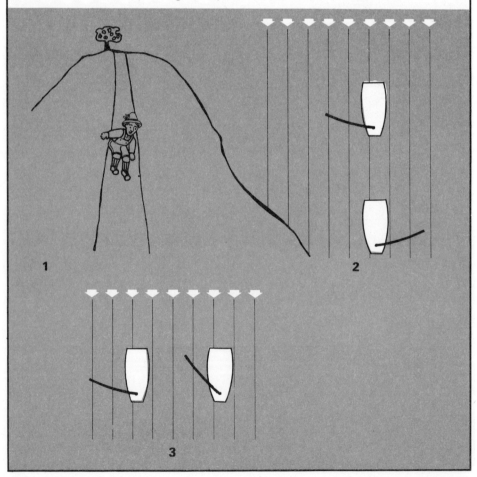

Making your sail pull well

To make sure your sail is pulling well which ever direction you are sailing, let it out until it begins to luff a bit. Then pull it in just until it stops luffing. Now your sail is adjusted properly and pulling well – and you'll go faster! Good sailors check their sails constantly to make sure they are pulling well.

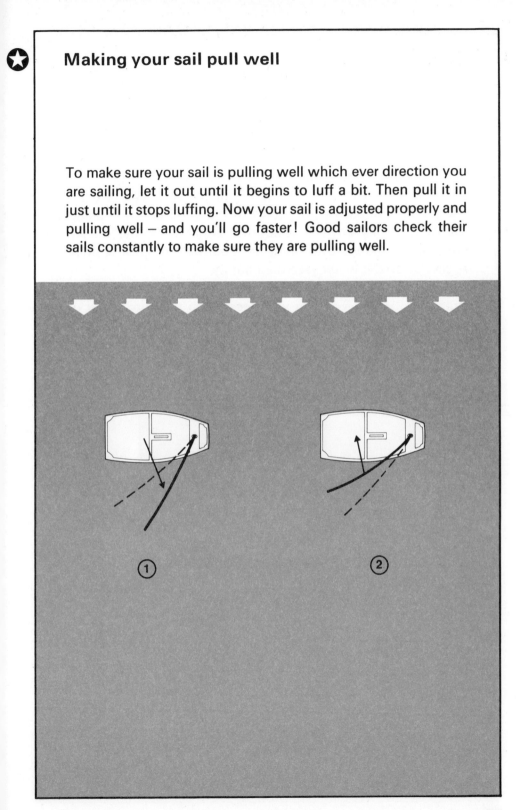

Heeling and hiking

In a strong wind the boat *heels* to leeward (see diagram 1); and if you are sitting in the centre of the boat your weight will not counterbalance the force of the wind which is filling the sail. The helmsman leans out of the boat to counterbalance the force of the wind to bring the boat up so that it is once again flat on the water (see diagram 2).

This is called hiking. Your boat must be equipped with straps into which you slip your feet when you are *hiking* or leaning way out of the boat (see diagram 3). These straps will hold you and help you regain your position in the boat when the puff of wind subsides.

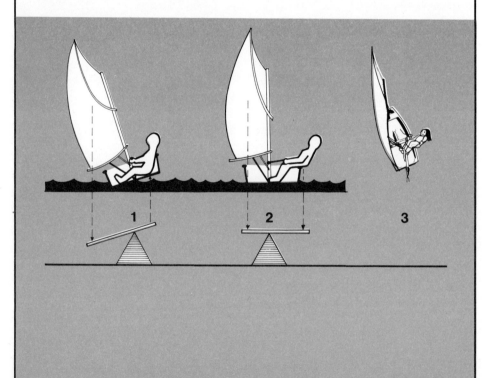

★ Heeling to windward

If the wind is very weak the boat may have a windward heel. You then have to sit in the middle or on the leeward side of the boat so the boat will be flat on the water.

Getting the most from your boat

Your boat will sail its best in the direction you wish:

1. When the sail is trimmed properly.

2. When your daggerboard is in the right position (down, to keep you from slipping sideways if you're beating; up, so not to slow you down when you're running).

3. When your weight is properly distributed. Your boat should be sailed *flat* on the water, so think about how far towards the bow or stern you sit as well as how far to windward or to leeward. You can steer from anywhere in your boat by using the tiller extension.

Regatta strategy

Make use of all your knowledge of sailing to help you win regattas. Here are some useful hints:
- Be in good physical condition.
- Rig your boat well.
- Make sure your sail is adjusted properly for the amount of wind blowing.
- For each point of sail make sure that the sail is in the most advantageous position to catch as much wind as possible.
- Cross the starting line just at the right moment.
- Aim correctly at the buoys, keeping to the shortest route possible.
- Don't lose track of the boats with which you are racing.
- Go around the buoys as closely as you can, but don't touch them. (See the sailing tip on page 93.)
- Lift your daggerboard ¾ out of the water when you are running with the wind so it doesn't slow you down (but don't forget to put it down again when you change direction).

Puffs of wind

Within a regular air current there are little puffs of wind, stronger than the main wind. By looking at the surface of the water in the direction from which the wind is coming you can see when one of these puffs is coming. A puff makes the water appear darker, and stirs it up into little waves or ripples which disappear when the puff passes.

Can you spot the puffs in this picture?

Pointing into the wind and easing off the wind

Pointing into the wind: This means to sail closer into the wind for a few seconds (to *point* closer to the direction from which the wind is coming). You use the tiller to *point up into the wind* when you see a strong puff coming from ahead. Some old sailors say: "In a puff, let her luff." You can also point closer into the wind from a running to a broad reach, from a broad reach to a beam reach and from a reach to a close haul.

Bearing off the wind: This means to head the boat slightly away from the direction that the wind is blowing. You can head off from a close haul to a beam reach, from a beam reach to a broad reach and from a broad reach to running. See the sailing tips on pages 95 and 96.

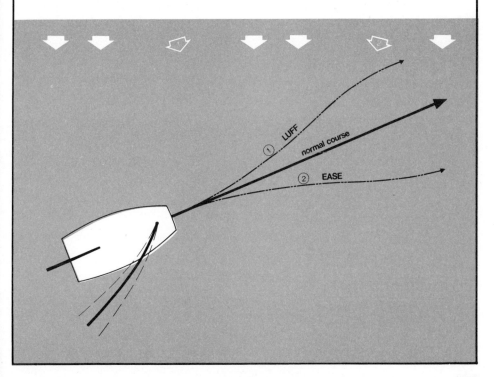

When it's windy and the puffs are stronger

If it's a windy day and the puffs are stronger, as well as pointing your boat up into the wind a bit with each puff you may need to hike out with each puff to keep your boat flat on the water. If a puff comes in very quickly and with considerable force, you can also ease the sheet out a bit to keep your boat upright.

By regulating your hiking position, adjusting your course and playing the sail (that is, constantly making sure it's pulling well), you'll be sailing your boat at its very best.

Obligations to commercial vessels

At some time or other you'll be sailing on the same waters as commercial vessels. You are expected to keep clear of them, as large vessels cannot easily be manoeuvred. You should make your change of course away from their direction very obvious to them.

Other types of boats

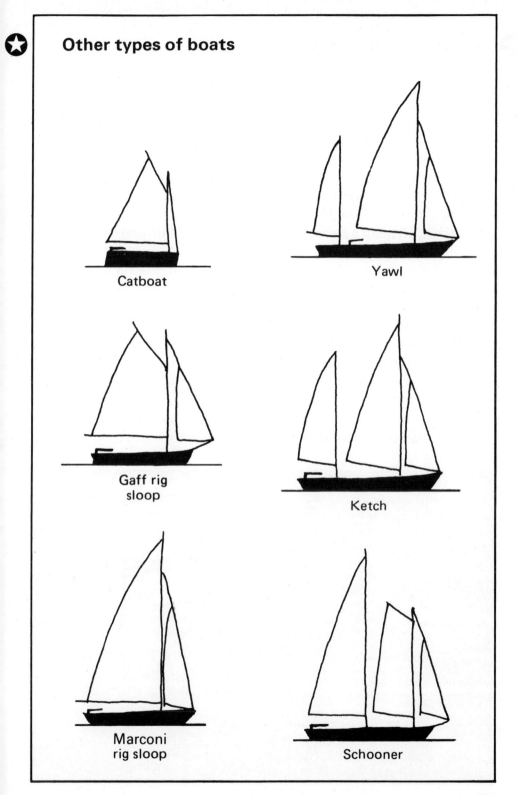

Catboat

Yawl

Gaff rig
sloop

Ketch

Marconi
rig sloop

Schooner

Setting sail from a dock

It's easy to set sail from a dock if you follow these simple steps:

1. Rig your boat on shore before taking it to the dock if you can. Check the wind direction and if you're not departing right away, tie your bow to the leeward side of the dock with the painter. (If there's a ring on the dock, a round turn and two half hitches is a good knot.)

2. Pull your boat alongside the dock to get in. Step in as near to the centre as you can and crouch low so the boat won't tip. Before you do this, make sure you have your life jacket on.

3. Attach your rudder and tiller.

4. Push down your daggerboard.

5. Check the wind direction again. Have someone untie your painter and throw it into your boat at the same time as they push your bow to allow you to sail away on a beam reach.

6. As soon as you are underway, sheet in so your sail pulls well and adjust your daggerboard to the correct position.

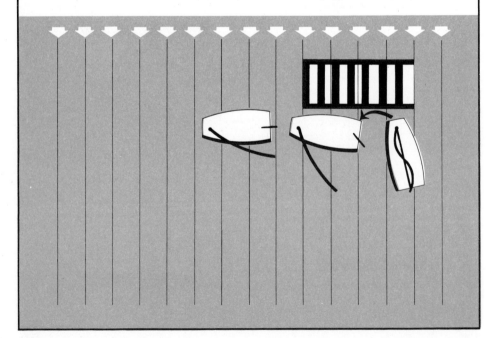

Getting back to a dock

This manoeuvre takes a little practice – best done when it's not too windy.

1. Approach the dock from its leeward side.

2. Ease the sheet a little and let the sail luff to slow you down.

3. When you're almost at the dock, turn sharply into the wind so that you are luffing. This stops you almost completely.

4. Let go of the sheet and grab the dock.

5. Tie the bow of your boat to the leeward side of the dock. Make sure your boat is not bumping into anything. If so, tie on some bumpers or put a line and anchor out to the stern.

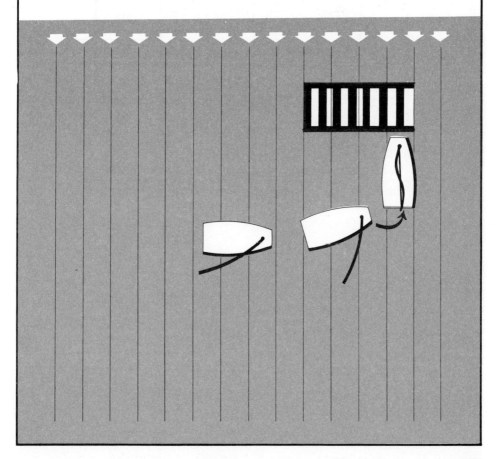

Regatta scoring

The winner is the one who has the least total points. Andrea placed 1st, 5th, 7th, 2nd, and 3rd, for a total of *31.7 points*. John placed 2nd, 7th, 9th, 1st, and 4th for a total of *39 points*. Andrea is the winner.

participants	result					total
Andrea	1	5	7	2	3	31.7
John	2	7	9	1	4	39
George	3	1	10	8	2	38.7
Patricia	5	3	11	4	5	50.7
Dianne	7	10	15	3	1	55.7

POSITION	1	2	3	4	5	6	7	8	9	10
POINTS	0.	3.	5.7	8.	10.	11.7	13.	14.	15.	16.

EXERCISE 31:
Gybing

Indicate with a "G" on the diagram below where it was necessary to gybe.

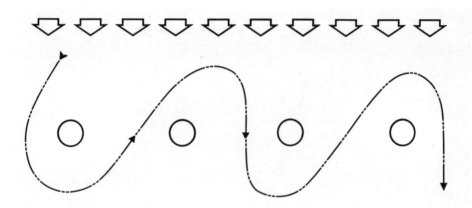

EXERCISE 32:
Sheltered areas

These are areas where there is no wind; they are in the lee of something. You must avoid these areas if you wish to keep moving. Place a cross (X) on the sheltered spots in the drawing below.

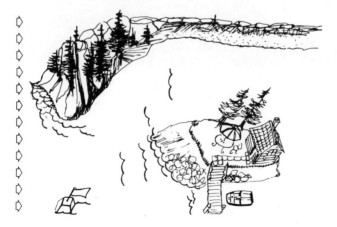

EXERCISE 33:
Sailing to windward and sailing downwind

Which boats are going upwind (windward)? Which boats are going downwind (with the wind)?

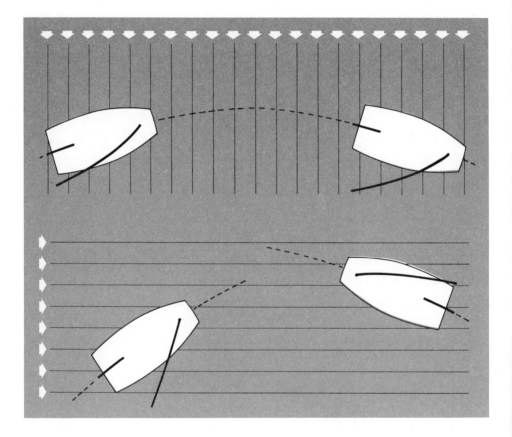

EXERCISE 34:
Pointing into the wind, easing off the wind

Write the words "pointing" or "easing" whenever they apply on the following course.

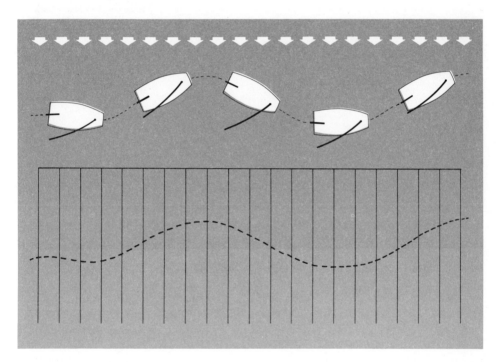

EXERCISE 35:
Capsizing and righting a boat

You're over! But don't worry. It's easy to get righted again. The pictures here show you how. After you've capsized and righted your boat a few times it'll take you less than a minute to get back up again and underway. It's a good idea to practice dumping on calm days when the water is warm.

1. Make sure no lines are caught on the boom or tiller.

2. Swim around your boat to the daggerboard. Make sure it is all the way down, if not pull it down.

3. Push down on the daggerboard and, if necessary, stand on it while you grab the gunwale. This will right the boat.

4. Climb aboard near the stern. The tiller will swing towards you as you climb in — be careful not to get knocked on the nose!

5. Bail away . . . then sail away.

EXERCISE 36:
Right of way

Match the commands with the drawing below:

1. Buoy room!

2. Starboard tack has right of way.

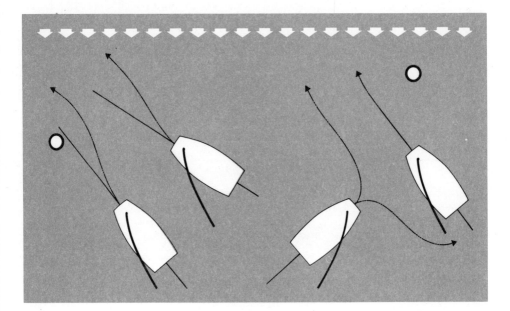

EXERCISE 37:
Quiz

1. Name three regulations determining right of way on the water.
2. What does beating mean?
3. Why is it necessary to sheet in a little when you point into the wind, and loosen the sheet when you ease off the wind?
4. Can you gybe without changing the direction of the boat?
5. What do you do when your dinghy "heels" too much?
6. Is it possible to see a puff of wind?

CHAPTER 5

Storing your dinghy

To keep your sailing dinghy clean and in good condition for a long time, you should put it away carefully after using it. If you have a safe spot to store your sailing gear it will be protected from the weather and be in good shape when you next need it.

1. To lower the sail, face your boat into the wind on the beach or dock. If you are with friends you can all work side by side in the landing area.

2. If your sail is wet, let it dry as it stands in the mast thwart, or remove it and take it inside and dry it on a special sail stand. A good sailor never folds a wet sail.

3. If you were sailing in salt water, rinse your sail in fresh water and let it dry.

4. Try not to fold your sail on the sand; the sand will act like sand-paper and damage the sail.

5. The illustration shows you how to fold your sail. You can leave the battens in their pockets. If your boat has a sprit sail (like the Optimist): a) Undo the downhaul from its cleat and leave the sail on the boom. b) Undo the figure 8 knot and remove the sheet from the block. c) Take down the sprit, letting it slide down the length of the mast. d) Take the mast out of the mast thwart.

6. Remove the wind indicator from the mast so that it won't get caught when you move the mast.

7. Store the rudder, daggerboard, bailing pail, wind indicator and any other equipment in the storage area of your house, summer camp or marina.

8. Clean the inside of the hull with a wet cloth to remove any sand or dirt.

9. Turn the hull over on the ground, or better yet on some old tires so that the air can circulate. You can then clean the bottom.

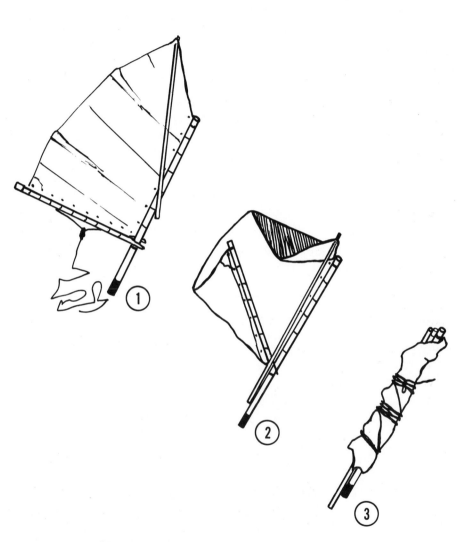

Important: Check the condition of all parts of your sailboat before you put them away. It's easier to repair problems when you first discover them. Further wear and tear may make fixing equipment impossible.

Winter storage

Because your dinghy is small it will easily fit in a garage or base-ment. You could even leave it outside during the winter as long as you turn it over and keep it off the ground. It could be placed on some old tires and covered with a large sheet of plastic.
Before you put your boat away for the year is a good time to check your buoyancy tanks. If you have air-filled tanks, pump air into them with a bicycle pump. Put liquid soap or detergent on all joints. If there are leaks, bubbles will form.
Note: Far better than air-filled buoyancy tanks are ones of solid monocellular styrofoam or polyethylene in a canvas bag. Never use kapok for buoyancy.

How to carry your dinghy

Bend your knees instead of your back when you are lifting your boat.

CHAPTER 6
Introduction to meteorology

Since you are making use of the wind to sail on the water, it is important that you know what weather is expected every time you set sail.

This chapter tells you how to keep track of the weather with meteorological instruments, and how to construct these instruments. It also tells you how to write a weather report.
Here are the main meteorological instruments:
• The *barometer* tells you what the present weather is, and in conjunction with other instruments, what the weather will be.
• The *thermometer* gives you the air temperature, telling you whether it's hot or cold out.
• The *hygrometer* or the *psychrometer* indicates the amount of humidity in the air.
• The *weather vane* indicates the direction of the wind.
• The *anemometer* gives you the speed or the force (intensity) of the wind.

Let's have a look at each of these devices, most of which you can make yourself. Then you can try the following experiments.

The barometer

Of all the instruments mentioned, the barometer is the most important to anyone who sails because it helps you to forecast the weather. You don't really need to know how it works, but as a sailor, you may find it interesting.

In order to understand how the barometer works we must first prove:
1. That air exists; 2. that air has weight; 3. that this weight is exerted upon us from top to bottom; 4. that the sun heats not the air, but the earth; 5. that hot air rises (it's light) and cold air falls (it's heavy).

1. Air exists

We breathe through our lungs the air which is found everywhere on the surface of the earth. Air carries sounds and smells. If there were no air you would not be able to hear people speak, nor could you smell the flowers.

Experiments

A. Shake your hands rapidly; you will feel the air between your fingers. What happens?

B. Blow up a balloon. What happens?

C. Invert an empty tumbler and push it into a bowl of water. What happens?

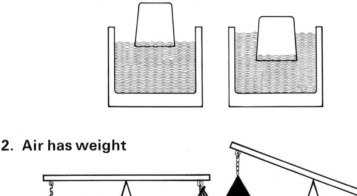

2. Air has weight

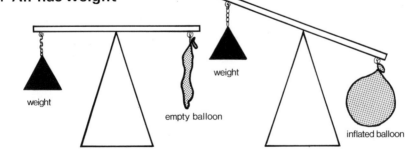

weight

empty balloon

weight

inflated balloon

3. The weight of air is exerted upon us from top to bottom

The bottom pancakes are flattened by the weight of those above. The same thing happens on the earth; *there is a lot of air at the earth's surface, much less as you go higher.*

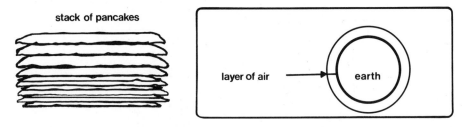

stack of pancakes

layer of air ——→ earth

4. The sun warms the earth and not the air

The rays of the sun penetrate the air layer to heat the earth and the large bodies of water.

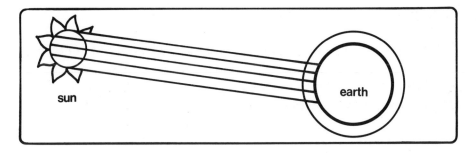

sun

earth

5. Warm air rises (it's light)
Cold air falls (it's heavy)

It is the earth and water, and not the sun, which heat the air. The hot air begins to rise. If it cools it begins to fall. Hot air masses bring bad weather while cold air masses bring good weather.

Experiments

A. Light a candle. It's just above the candle that the air is the hottest.

B. Look at a fireplace; the smoke is the hot air which rises.

C. Open a refrigerator; you will feel the cold at your feet.

History of the barometer

The barometer was invented by Toricelli. He filled a glass tube with mercury. He then blocked the end of the tube with his finger and inverted the tube in a tank half-filled with mercury.

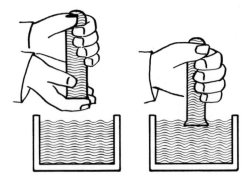

Why doesn't the mercury rush down into the tank ? The pressure or weight of the air exerted on the mercury in the tank prevents the mercury in the tube from flowing out.

The height of a column of mercury can be measured in inches, centimetres, millimetres or better yet in millibars (unit of atmospheric pressure). The normal atmospheric pressure is 29.9 inches, 760 millimetres or 1013 millibars of mercury.

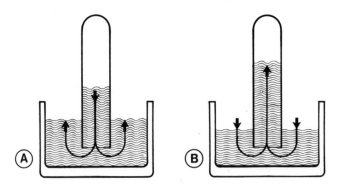

A) When the mercury in the tube goes *down*, the pressure on the mercury in the tank is less (warm air masses are light) indicating *bad weather*.

B) When the mercury in the tube *rises* the pressure on the mercury in the tank is more (cold air masses are heavy) indicating *good weather*.

How the barometer works

The barometer is a scale which measures the weight of the air (air pressure or atmospheric pressure). The barometer, no matter where it is located, whether it be in the house or outside, records the weight of the air which is directly above it.

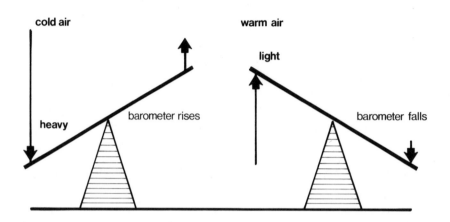

Commercial barometers

1. The most popular type of commercial barometer is the *aneroid*. This barometer has a moveable hand that you can set in the same position as the indicator of the barometer. You can then determine whether the barometer is rising or falling by comparing the new position of the indicator with the setting of the hand.

2. The *barograph* is a precision barometer. The atmospheric pressure is recorded daily on a sheet of graph paper (barogram).

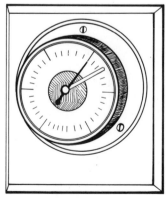
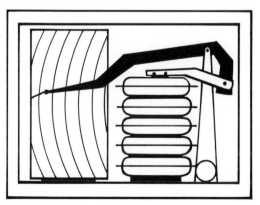

Aneroid barometer   Barograph

How to make a barogram

Use a large piece of cardboard to make a barogram like the one illustrated here.

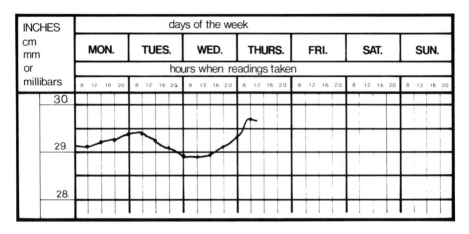

INCHES cm mm or millibars	days of the week						
	MON.	TUES.	WED.	THURS.	FRI.	SAT.	SUN.
	hours when readings taken						
	8 12 16 20	8 12 16 20	8 12 16 20	8 12 16 20	8 12 16 20	8 12 16 20	8 12 16 20
30.							
29.							
28.							

Each day, at the indicated times, mark a dot on the line to represent the figure indicated by the barometer. You can then draw a line to join each of these dots. To find out what this line will tell you, read the paragraphs on the interpretation of the barogram on the opposite page.

Interpretation of your barogram

Look at the sample graphs in each of the numbered squares and read the paragraph below with the corresponding number.

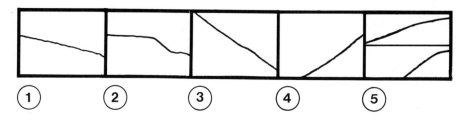

Remember that a falling barometer means bad weather – rain, wind, storms and heat, and a rising barometer means fair weather – no rain but colder.

1. A slow, steady drop in barometric pressure (3 or 4 millimetres in 24 hours) means that there is a low-pressure area in the distance. Often there is no noticeable change in the weather.

2. A sudden drop in barometric pressure, even if it is slight (2 or 3 millimetres in 2 or 3 hours) always means that there is some disturbance nearby. Generally this means that there will be short squalls and showers. If it is a large drop (8 to 10 millimetres in 5 or 6 hours) there will be strong winds and storms.

3. A large, steady drop in pressure indicates that there will be a long spell of bad weather. This will mean a noticeable change in the weather because the barometer has dropped so far.

4. An abrupt rise in the barometer when the weather is fine and the pressure is near average means that a low-pressure area is advancing which will cause the barometer to drop.

5. A rapid rise in air pressure when the barometer is low means a short spell of good weather, but if the rise is large and steady there will be a longer period of fair weather.

You can see now that what is important is not the barometric reading itself, but the *trend* of the barometer to rise or fall *rapidly* or *steadily*. The weather forecast provided for you by your barogram is good only for the following 6 hours.

In the drawing below you see a barogram made by the barograph during the week of December 3 to 9, 1973. (For each rise and fall of the barometer we have indicated the paragraph number of the correct interpretation from the preceding page.)

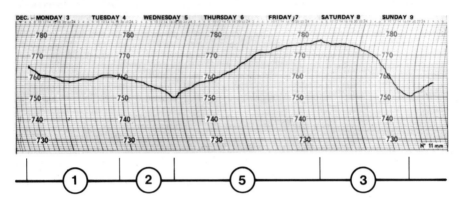

Can you interpret the barograms opposite?

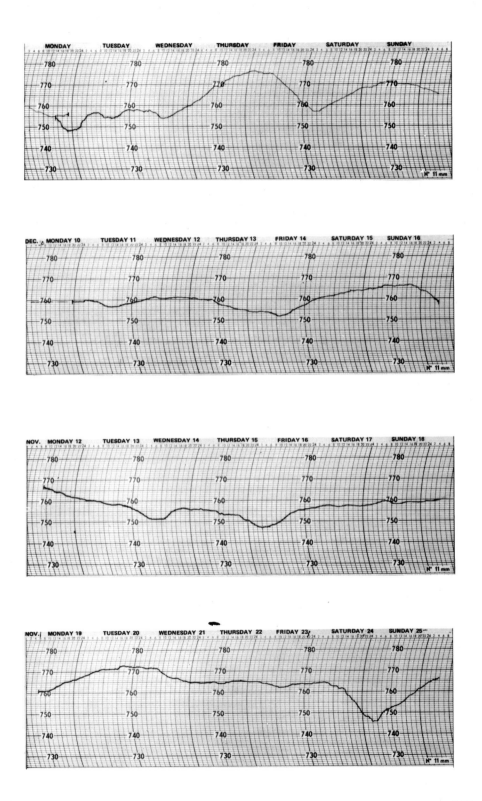

129

The hygrometer

There is humidity in the air. Humidity is evaporated water; this invisible water in the air is called water vapour. When there is not enough humidity in the air the skin on our hands and our lips becomes dry and chapped.
When there is too much humidity in the air we feel uncomfortable, listless and tired.

How the hygrometer works: The hair of a horse helps us to determine how much humidity is in the air. When there is a lot of water vapour in the air the horsehair stretches. When there is not much water vapour in the air the horsehair shrinks.

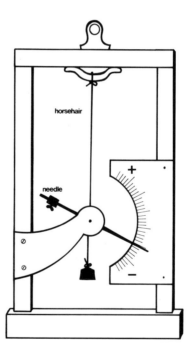

One hygrometer
The horsehair is stretched when there is a lot of water vapour in the air and the needle moves upward. When the amount of water vapour in the air decreases the hair shrinks and the needle swings downward.

Other hygrometers

The following hygrometers all work like the previous one.

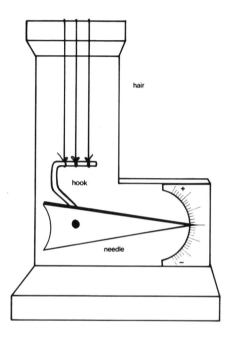

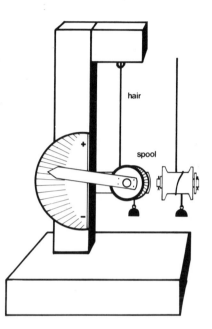

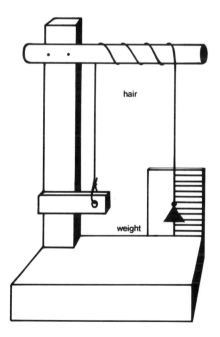

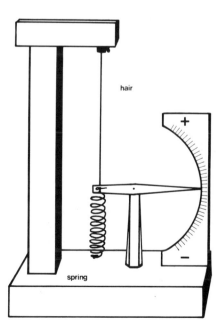

The thermometer

The *thermometer* measures the degree of heat in the air or water.

How it works: The mercury in an enclosed glass tube rises when it is warm and drops when it is cool. It's like the track of a railroad; when it's warm it stretches, and when it's cold it shrinks.

Some thermometers are filled with alcohol instead of mercury to measure very low temperatures.

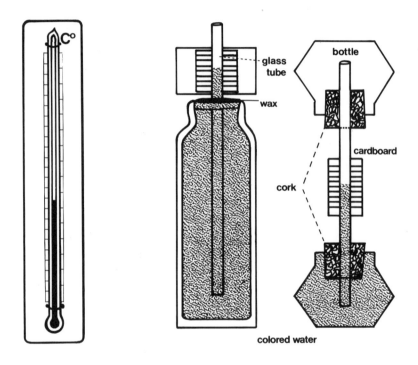

colored water

How a thermometer is constructed

Experiment

Make a thermometer similar to one of those shown above. Place it in a bowl of melting ice and mark a "0" at the level of the coloured water.

Next place the thermometer over the steam from boiling water and mark "100" at the level of the coloured water.

Divide the space between 0 and 100 into equal parts. You now have a Celsius thermometer.

The psychrometer

This is another device used to measure the amount of humidity in the air. It gives us an exact indication.

How it works: Two mercury thermometers are placed side by side. One of them is wrapped in a little piece of cheesecloth which rests in a dish of water.

By wetting the thermometer on the left you get 100 per cent humidity. The other thermometer, which has not been wetted, will be affected only by the invisible water vapour present in the air.

Stir up the air around the psychrometer by fanning it with a book or a piece of cardboard, and compare the two thermometers to see if there is a lot of humidity in the air.

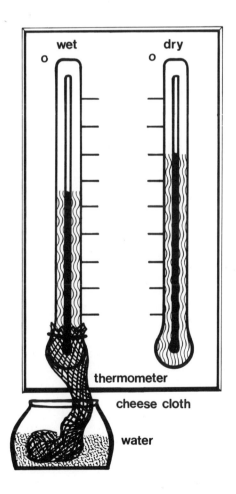

Psychrometric table

If there is a *wide spread* between the two columns of mercury there is not much humidity in the air. If, on the other hand, both columns of mercury are at the same level there is a lot of humidity in the air.

To obtain a precise reading of the percentage of humidity in the air, subtract the reading of the wet thermometer from the reading of the dry thermometer and find the answer on the psychrometric table.

Example: Wet thermometer 25°C   Dry thermometer 30°C
Difference   dry-wet = 30 − 25 = 5

Look for the figure 5 in the horizontal line across the top of the psychrometric table. Look for the figure 30 in the vertical column to the left of the psychrometric table. Move down under the 5 and across beside the 30 until the two lines come together at 64% − very humid.

PSYCHROMETRIC TABLE
TABLE OF PERCENTAGES OF HUMIDITY

Temperature of the dry thermometer (° celsius)	Variation (difference) between the temperatures of the two thermometers (in degrees)														
	0.0	0.5	1.0	1.5	2.0	2.5	3.0	3.5	4.0	4.5	5.0	5.5	6.0	6.5	7.0
0	100%	90	80	71	63	56	49	43	37	32	28	23	20	16	13
1	100	90	81	72	65	58	51	45	40	35	30	26	22	19	16
2	100	90	82	74	66	59	53	47	42	37	33	29	25	22	19
3	100	91	82	75	67	61	55	49	44	39	35	31	27	24	21
4	100	91	83	75	66	62	56	51	46	41	37	33	30	26	24
5	100	91	84	76	70	64	58	53	48	43	39	35	32	29	26
6	100	92	84	77	71	65	59	54	49	45	41	37	34	31	28
7	100	92	85	78	72	65	61	56	51	47	43	39	36	33	30
8	100	92	85	79	73	67	62	57	52	48	44	41	37	34	32
9	100	93	86	79	74	68	63	58	54	50	46	42	39	36	33
10	100	93	86	80	74	69	64	59	55	51	47	44	41	38	35
11	100	93	87	81	75	70	65	60	56	52	49	45	42	39	36
12	100	93	87	81	76	71	66	61	57	54	50	47	43	41	38
13	100	94	87	82	76	71	67	62	58	55	51	48	45	42	39
14	100	94	88	82	77	72	68	63	59	56	52	49	46	43	40
15	100	94	88	83	78	73	68	64	60	57	53	50	47	44	42
16	100	94	88	83	78	74	69	65	61	58	54	51	48	45	43
17	100	94	89	83	79	74	70	66	62	59	55	52	49	46	44
18	100	94	89	84	79	75	70	67	63	59	56	53	50	47	45
19	100	94	89	84	80	75	71	67	63	60	57	54	51	48	46
20	100	95	89	85	80	76	72	68	64	61	58	55	52	49	47
21	100	95	90	85	80	76	72	68	65	62	58	55	53	50	47
22	100	95	90	85	81	77	73	69	66	62	59	56	53	51	48
23	100	95	90	86	81	77	73	70	66	63	60	57	54	52	49
24	100	95	90	86	82	78	74	70	67	63	60	58	55	52	50
25	100	95	90	86	82	78	74	71	67	64	61	58	56	53	50
26	100	95	91	86	82	79	75	71	68	65	62	59	56	54	51
27	100	95	91	87	83	79	75	72	68	65	62	59	57	54	52
28	100	95	91	87	83	79	75	72	69	66	63	60	57	55	52
29	100	95	91	87	83	79	76	72	69	66	63	60	58	55	53
30	100	96	91	87	83	80	76	73	70	67	64	61	58	56	53
31	100	96	91	87	83	80	76	73	70	67	64	61	59	56	54
32	100	96	91	88	84	80	77	73	70	67	65	62	59	57	54
33	100	96	92	88	84	80	77	74	71	68	65	62	60	57	55
34	100	96	92	88	84	81	77	74	71	68	65	63	60	58	55
35	100	96	92	88	84	81	78	74	71	68	66	63	61	58	56

The weather vane

This instrument tells us where the wind is coming from. Once we know this we also know the direction of the wind, or where it's going.

Example: If the weather vane tells us that the wind is coming from the south, that means it is moving from south to north; it is called a south wind.

Wind is air in motion.

When the air is warmed by the earth or by the water, it rises (1). When the air is cooled by the earth or water it falls from the height to which it had previously risen (2).

Does the *warm* air which is rising leave an empty space underneath (3)?

Does the *cold* air which is falling leave an empty space above (4)? Here is what happens: the cold air falls to fill the empty space created by the warm air which is rising. The colder air in the form wind is pulled towards the space (vacuum) left by the rising warm air (5).

the empty space (vacuum) left by the cold air (6).

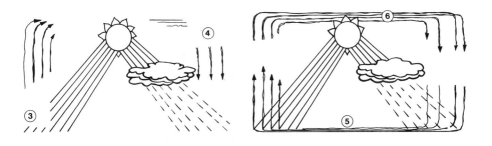

Some types of weather vanes

The compass

You can indicate on your weather vane the four cardinal points of the compass – north, south, east and west, and the four secondary points – north west, north east, south east, and south west.

You must orient your weather vane. Find north on a compass and line it up with the north on your weather vane. This helps you to be more precise in determining the direction of the wind.

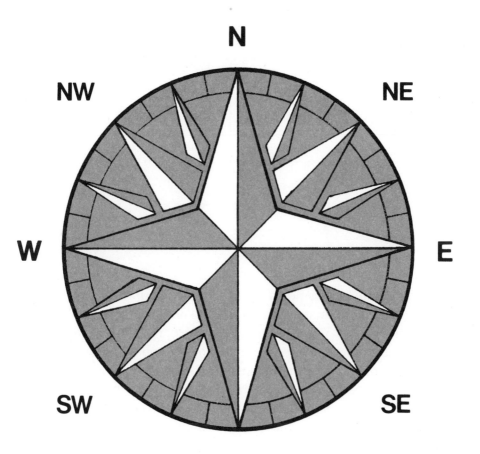

The anemometer

The anemometer indicates wind speed.

Anemometer 1
How it works: The wind blows and turns the four cones or half-spheres. At each turn the counting strip of plastic, leather, or flexible wood, hits and passes the horizontal wooden stick attached to the main support. Each time the strip passes the stick there will be a little click.

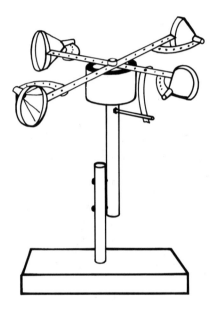

To determine the wind speed in miles per hour or kilometres per hour ask a parent or instructor to take you and your anemometer for a car ride one day when there is *no wind*. You will need a stop watch. Hold the anemometer out the window and count the number of clicks per minute at different speeds. Record the number of clicks per minute at each speed on a sheet of paper, this will be your wind speed chart. Whenever you want to know the wind speed at a certain location, set up the anemometer, count the clicks per minute and find the corresponding speed from your chart.

Anemometer 2

This anemometer is rather delicate and should not be left outside. To calculate the wind speed do what you did for Anemometer number 1.

When you are taking wind speed readings place the anemometer in an open spot, at least 1½ metres from the ground. *Be careful not to block the wind by getting in front of the anemometer.*

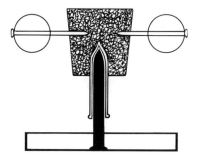

The ventimeter

The ventimeter is also used to determine wind speed, but in a different way.

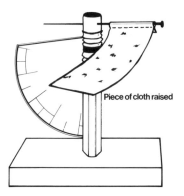

Piece of cloth raised

How it works: As the wind blows the piece of cloth is raised. When there is a strong wind it is almost horizontal; when the wind drops it hangs vertically.

There are many kinds of ventimeters on sale in shops selling precision instruments. They are all practical and easy to use. They can be slipped into a pocket, and will give you the wind speed at a glance.

The Beaufort Wind Force Scale

In 1808 Sir Francis Beaufort a British admiral found a way to simplify the recording of the speed or force of the wind. He put a number beside different approximate wind speeds ranging from 0 for complete calm to 12 for a hurricane. This numbered code was later revised to reflect the actual speed of the wind as measured by an anemometer. It has been a useful guide to sailors ever since.

The chart below tells you how to identify the various Beaufort wind force numbers:

Beaufort Number (Force)	Official Description	WIND SPEED		
		knots	km per hour	Miles per hour
0	calm	1	1	1
1	light air	1 - 3	1 - 5	1 - 3
2	light breeze	4 - 6	6 - 11	4 - 7
3	gentle breeze	7 - 10	12 - 19	8 - 12
4	moderate breeze	11 - 16	20 - 28	13 - 18
5	fresh breeze	17 - 21	29 - 38	19 - 24
6*	strong breeze	22 - 27	39 - 49	25 - 31
7	near gale	28 - 33	50 - 61	32 - 38
8	gale	34 - 40	62 - 74	39 - 46
9	strong gale	41 - 47	75 - 88	47 - 54
10	storm	48 - 55	89 - 102	55 - 63
11	violent storm	56 - 65	103 - 117	64 - 75
12	hurricane	64 or more	118 or more	78 or more

*Maximum wind for small boats

Effects of the wind on land	Effects of the wind on the water
Smoke rises vertically.	The water is like a mirror — perfectly calm.
Smoke indicates the direction of the wind, but weather vanes do not move.	There are ripples on the water with the appearance of scales.
You can feel wind on your face. Leaves rustle and weather vanes are moved by the wind.	Small more defined wavelets appear. Crests of wavelets are transparent and do not break.
Leaves and small twigs move constantly. A light flag waves.	Very small waves with crests that are beginning to break appear. Some foam. A few whitecaps (or horses as they are called by sailors).
Dust, papers blow about. Small branches move.	Longer small waves. More frequent whitecaps.
Small trees or shrubs begin to sway in the wind.	Moderate sized waves, longer. Many whitecaps and perhaps some spray.
Large branches sway. Telephone wires whistle. It's difficult to use an umbrella.	Large waves beginning to form. Many whitecaps and some spray.
Large trees are in motion. It's difficult to walk against the wind.	The white foam from breaking waves begins to blow in streaks along the direction of the wind.
The wind breaks small branches from trees.	Spray swirls from swells. Foam is blown in well-marked streaks along the direction of the wind.
Some damage to roofs, chimneys, tv antennaes, tiles, shingles can occur.	High waves, crests begin to break in rollers. Spray may reduce visibility.
Seldom experienced inland. Trees are uprooted. Considerable damage to buildings.	Huge waves with overhanging crests. Foam blown in dense white streaks along the water and the sea looks almost white. Visibility is reduced.
Very rare. Causes widespread damage.	Extremely high waves. The sea is covered with long white patches of foam. Visibility reduced.
Destruction of nearly all property.	The air is filled with foam and spray. There is almost no visibility. The sea is completely white with driving spray.

The meteorological cycle

The sun (1) warms the water (2). The invisible water vapour (3) rises and becomes visible as soon as it is cooled (4). This vapour forms clouds (5) which become laden with water which falls as rain (6).

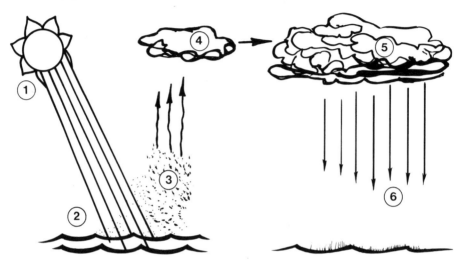

You can prove that this cycle exists right in your kitchen. Boil some water in a kettle; watch the water vapour or steam rise; hold a cold spoon in the steam. When the steam hits the cold spoon, water will become a liquid again.

142

Clouds

Clouds are made up of very tiny water droplets.

There are many kinds of clouds. Here are a few of them and some information about what they mean to you as a sailor.

Cirrocumulus clouds are very high clouds. If they appear in little waves in the sky this is called a "mackerel sky". A mackerel sky can mean rain within a few days.

Cirrostratus clouds are also very high clouds usually like a thin veil covering most of the sky. They are often seen before the barometer falls.

Cumulonimbus cloud   Large cumulus cloud

Cumulonimbus are like anvils in the sky — dark clouds which hang low over the land or sea.

Large cumulus rain clouds are heavy, bumpy clouds (like clumps of cotton batting).

When you see cumulonimbus or large cumulus clouds it is best not to sail. Or return to shore quickly if you are already on the water.

If there is a sudden calm, if the wind drops completely or the sky darkens, head for shore immediately.

How to make your own weather bulletin

1. Time: 8 o'clock in the morning is written 0800 hours.
2 o'clock in the afternoon is written: $1200 + 200 = 1400$ hours.
8 o'clock in the evening is written: $1200 + 800 = 2000$ hours.

2. Falling rapidly ⊡ ; falling slowly ◗ ; rising rapidly ⊡ ; rising slowly ◸ .

3. Cloud formations: write in the numbers of the cloud types according to the chart available from the National Weather Service. You can obtain a copy of this chart by writing to the National Weather Service, 30 Rockefeller Plaza, New York, New York 10020.

4. Clear sky □ ; ¼ cloud cover ◖ ; ½ cloud cover ◨ ; ¾ cloud cover ◩ ; completely overcast ■ .

WEATHER REPORT

Location: (lake, camp, dock etc.) . . . .
Name: . . . . **Date:** . . . . **Time:**[1] . . . .

Barometer: Pressure:[2] . . . rising. . . . .stable . . . . falling. . . . .
Temperature: °C . . . .
Humidity: (%) . . . .
Cloud Formations:[3] . . . .
Direction of the wind: . . . .
Wind Speed: . . . .
Present Weather: (rain, wind, fog etc.) . . . .
Condition of the sky:[4] . . . .
Forecast for the next 6 hours: . . . .
. . . .
. . . .
. . . .

Quiz

True or false

1. Air has weight . . . .

2. The device used to measure atmospheric pressure is the psychrometer . . . .

3. The greater the variation between the readings of the thermometers of a psychrometer, the more humidity there is in the air . . . .

4. The liquid in a mercury thermometer expands when it's warm and contracts when it's cold . . . .

5. The head of the arrow on the weather vane indicates in which direction the wind is blowing . . . .

6. When it's humid our hair stretches . . . .

7. It is important to consider the direction of the wind when interpreting barometric readings . . . .

8. Cumulus clouds resemble horses in the sky . . . .

9. Wind is air in motion, caused by the presence of warm and cold air masses . . . .

Underline the right answer

1. The mercury barometer was invented by:

    a) Torricelli

    b) Galileo

    c) Celsius

2. The most important part of the hygrometer is:

    a) humidity

    b) an indicator

    c) the hair

3. Cold air which moves in to fill the vacuum created by the rise of warm air is called:

    a) humidity

    b) temperature

    c) wind

4. The best device for measuring the humidity in the air is:
   a) a hair
   b) a horsehair
   c) a thread
5. Instead of using an anemometer you could use:
   a) a ventimeter
   b) a weather vane
   c) a sun dial
6. To calculate the percentage of humidity in the air you must read:
   a) the dry thermometer of a psychrometer
   b) the difference between the dry thermometer and the wet thermometer
   c) the wet thermometer of a psychrometer

Draw a line from the word in the column on the left to an associated word in the column on the right

1. barometer	**a)** humidity
2. cumulonimbus	**b)** Torricelli
3. hygrometer	**c)** hurricane
4. anometer	**d)** sailing dinghy
5. Optimist	**e)** rain

How's your weather eye?

Look at the picture opposite. What do you think the Beaufort wind force would be? The answer is on page 171.

CHAPTER 7
Dressing for sailing

When it's cold
1. woollen turtle-neck sweater
2. rubber rain jacket
3. warm pants under waterproof (rubberized) pants
4. warm socks
5. rubber boots or shoes
6. sailing gloves

When it's warm
1. sun lotion or barrier cream (to keep you from burning)
2. light sweater or cotton shirt
3. bathing suit
4. sneakers or canvas sport shoes (to protect the inside of the boat and to keep you from slipping).

CHAPTER 8
Good food for sailors

You need foods which give you energy: rice, corn, potatoes, cereals and grains, bananas, dates, figs, oranges, mandarin oranges, honey, sugar, chocolate, jams.

You need foods for body building: grilled light meats, beef, eggs, fish, mushrooms, string beans, other kinds of beans (kidney, lima, etc.), peas, spinach, carrots, cabbage, lettuce.

There are certain essential foods which give you minerals and vitamins: butter, leafy green vegetables, carrots, radishes, raw fruit, raw vegetables.

Recommended drinks include water, natural fruit juices and milk.

CHAPTER 9
Keeping in shape

Top sailors keep in good physical condition to prepare themselves for sailing in bad weather or competing in regattas.

Chances are you are already in fine shape. Here are a few good exercises for sailing. See how you can do them. Don't do too many of each one at a time and stop when you are tired.

Warm-ups

1. Start with some running and jumping, then limber up your spine with:

2. arched and rounded back

3. the Moslem prayer

4. raising and lowering knees while on back

Exercises

Stomach

These exercises require more effort if the legs are bent.

1. Hiking position – sitting on the ground, hips as close as possible to heels, feet held under a piece of furniture. Do not lie back on the floor, touch only head or shoulder.

Torso

Choose one of the three exercises shown.

2. Same position as for exercise 1, twist as you come up, touching right shoulder to left knee and vice-versa.

3. Same starting position: go back only 45°, hands behind head, twist to touch elbow to floor.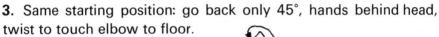

4. Standing, hands behind neck, bend from side to side at the waist.

Legs

5. Standing, legs astride, bend down to the right, touching your hip to your right heel, keeping the back straight. Come back to the upright position and repeat to the left.

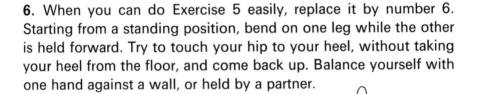

6. When you can do Exercise 5 easily, replace it by number 6. Starting from a standing position, bend on one leg while the other is held forward. Try to touch your hip to your heel, without taking your heel from the floor, and come back up. Balance yourself with one hand against a wall, or held by a partner.

Back

7. Standing, legs astride and bent. Back flat, at a 45° angle, hands behind neck, twist from side to side, watching elbows move back.

Arms

8. Climb a rope, holding knees high. Work at coming down the rope, hand over hand (climb a little higher each time you do the exercise).

Cool off

Monkey slumps. Place your feet apart, bend your knees. Put your hands on your knees and let them slide off and drop to the floor. Relax.

CHAPTER 10
Looking after your sailing dinghy

To keep your dinghy looking attractive and in good working condition you should, at least once a year, apply varnish or polyurethane to the mast, sprit, boom, rudder and daggerboard. This might be a good job for a long winter afternoon.

If your boat has a wooden hull you should check once a year to see if it needs repainting or revarnishing. You should always sand (with fine sandpaper) the parts you are going to paint or varnish.

Before using an electric sander make sure there is an adult present to advise you about the precautions that must be taken with electric equipment.

Here's what you will need
an old shirt for protection
a brush 2 inches (5 cm) wide
fine sandpaper
water for soaking sandpaper if you use wet-or-dry sandpaper
paint, varnish or polyurethane, and turpentine or thinner
old newspapers to spread under your work
old rags or paper towel to clean up

What to do

1. Set yourself up in a well-ventilated, sheltered spot.

2. Remove the sail from the mast, boom, sprit combination so it won't get dirty.

3. Set up two supports or saw horses for the things you are going to sand.

4. Put old newspapers on the floor to protect it.

5. You must now sand the mast, the boom and the sprit until the wood is very smooth. Wet your sandpaper when it becomes dirty. You will know you have done a good job if the mast, boom and sprit feel completely smooth when you run your fingers over them.

6. Wipe the pieces with a cloth to take off any dust.

7. Put on the first coat of varnish or paint. *Warning*: Do not put on a thick first coat. A thick coat will run or wrinkle and you'll have to start again.

8. Each time that you take some paint or varnish on your brush squeeze it against the side of the can to remove the excess.

9. Wait until the first coat is thoroughly dry before you apply the second. You could even sand lightly between coats.

10. When you are finished, clean your brush in turpentine or thinner so that the bristles will not harden making it impossible to use again. You should rinse your brush several times and wipe it with newspapers or rags. An adult should be present while you are doing this.

CHAPTER 11
Making a miniature sailboat

In the wintertime when you can't sail your boat, you might want to build a miniature sailboat of cardboard, plasticine, clay, balsa wood or even plywood to remind you of fun to come in the summer. You will find patterns for the pieces you'll need on the following pages. Depending on the material you use, you can make a boat that will really sail.

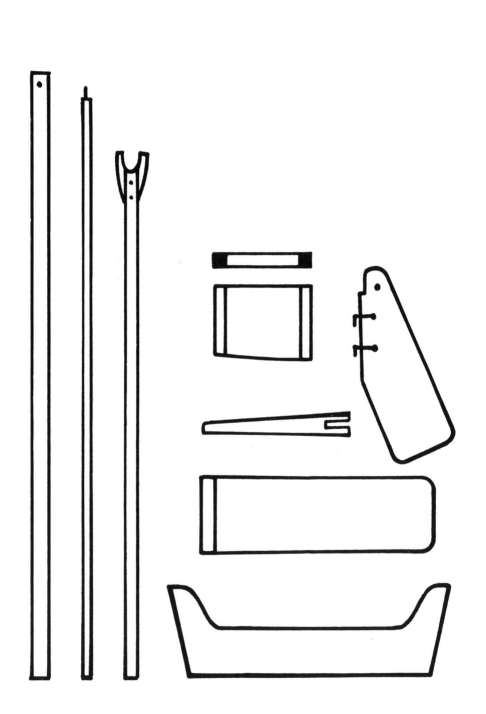

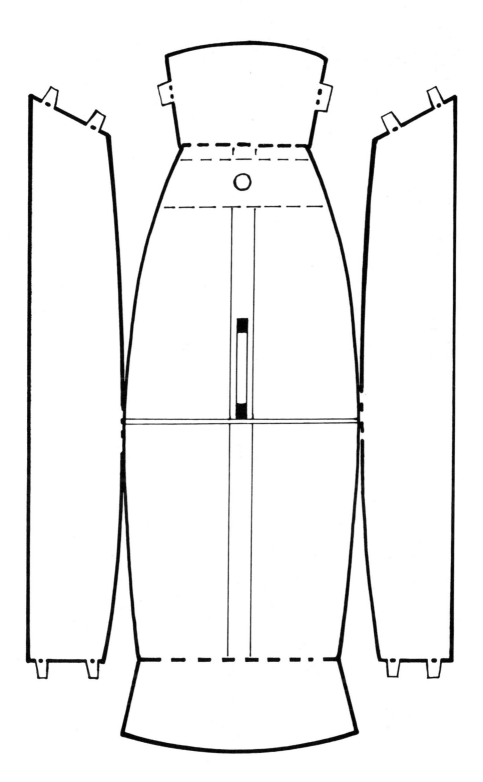

CHAPTER 12
Making a sailboat mobile

You will need some walnut shells, construction paper in different colours, black thread, small sticks (about $2\frac{1}{2}$ inches or 7 cm long), thin metal or wooden rods and glue.

What to do
1. Split the walnuts into two.
2. Eat the insides!
3. Glue the masts to the bottom of the narrow part of the shell.
4. Cut the sails out of the coloured construction paper, and stick them on the masts.
5. Make a nick or a hole in the end of the mast for the thread. Use glue if necessary.
6. Attach the boats to the rods. Tie them on with a clove hitch.
7. Eat the remaining nuts.

CHAPTER 13
Advice for parents and instructors

Perhaps you are anxious about sending a youngster out alone on the water in a small sailboat? There is little cause to worry; sailing dinghies have been used with great success in many junior sailing classes, and the method of teaching adopted in this manual makes it easy for any young person to control and understand his boat.

As you watch your youngsters learning to sail you may find that you also are becoming interested in sailing. The same small craft suggested here for use by your children are also suitable for you; they are streamlined and light, yet they are true sailing boats. The sailing theory described here applies equally to large and small boats – as both utilize the wind in the same way. Later, if you wish to purchase a larger boat, your knowledge of sailing and small craft will help you to choose the most suitable one for your family.

This manual deals primarily with the essentials of sailing. Because it is written so that a child may understand the basic principles, it will be easy for you, as a parent or supervisor, to learn to sail at the same time.

The section beginning on the next page will answer questions you may have and gives you guidelines for measuring your youngster's progress. It is important that you read this section before your child begins working through the chapters.

Supervising sailing

Age limit

There is no age limit for sailing; if children are quite young (6, 7, or 8 years) the practice courses suggested here can be shorter and the sailing can be done only when the wind is Force 1 or 2 (see pages 140 and 141). Those responsible for the safety of younger children should be well trained and alert. Of course, younger children are not expected to be as technically competent as the older ones.

Learning period

It is very important to adapt the learning process to the age and skills of youngsters. The length of the learning period will vary depending on how the course outlined in this book is used, but it is essential that each *lesson* contain a session on the water, and some related sailing theory.

The principal objective of this book is to instill in each beginner the desire to sail; therefore most of each lesson should be devoted to actual sailing on the water. The practice sessions on the water can be supplemented by the games outlined on page 171, which allow the youngsters to practice the techniques without being overly conscious of them.

If more than one youngster is involved it is a good idea to put beginners and experienced youngsters in the same group; the experienced ones can be responsible for certain parts of the lesson, such as preparation of the equipment or surveillance of the activities. A child can benefit from watching the way others do things; many questions can be answered by observation.

Usually you will find that you have half a day, a whole day, or perhaps a week to teach sailing to a group of children. If you have very little time you can provide only a general idea of essential techniques, while devoting most of the time to practice on the water. If there is more time available obviously more related areas can be explored. It's a good idea not to concentrate on any one area for an extended period of time; include other activities (meteorology, crafts, boat-building, swimming and diving, nature walks, etc.) so that children do not become tired or bored.

Organization of group lessons

There should be two instructors per group of ten students. The two instructors or parents should be on the shore to help the youngsters rig their dinghies. Before the dinghies set sail the instructors should check the rescue boat and take it out to buoy number 1, so that they may watch the students complete the practice course. When the youngsters return to shore, two instructors should be there ahead of them to make sure that each boat has its daggerboard up.

It is highly recommended that the instructors be master swimmers or lifeguards since there is the possibility they will have to deal with an aquatic emergency.

If there is a large group of learners it is a good idea to have an assistant on the spot to answer telephone calls and handle unforeseen events.

Equipment
A) Boats
· 10 sailing dinghies for every two instructors, each one equipped with a painter, a paddle and a bailing pail tied into the boat.

B) Safety
· well constructed headquarters (cabin, office, lounge, etc.)
· a telephone and important numbers (Fire, Police, Ambulance)
· a first-aid kit
· a rescue boat with an outboard motor of at least 10 horsepower.

A suitable rescue boat might be an inflatable, stabilized rubber dinghy. This way there will be no risk of damaging collisions, and the rubber boat can be used to support and empty a capsized sailboat. It also provides a recognizable waymark on the water for beginning sailors.
· field glasses
· a whistle
· a small-boat weather warning signal (standardized warning flags are available)

C) Teaching

On the water:
- whistle and extra life jacket (kept in the rescue boat)
- band-aids
- rope, anchor, bailing pail
- knife
- loudspeaker (you can lose your voice quickly by shouting)
- three or more buoys with nylon flags attached (see page 175)

On the shore:
- quiet quarters close to the waterfront and overlooking it if possible where students and teachers can relax and talk about sailing
- dressing room
- black board
- tables and chairs for writing and craft work
- wooden models of sailing dinghies
- lengths of rope for knot tying
- beach area for boat storage
- inside storage area to hang sails and store rudders and dagger-boards

D) Clothing

Instructors and parents must be responsible for seeing that young-sters are properly dressed (see Chapter 7). Children who are chilled may suffer from cramps and dizziness, and will lose interest in sailing all together.

Entrance requirements

The boats suggested in this book (the Optimist in particular) are very safe, and have been used with great success in children's sailing classes. Nonetheless, children who are learning to sail should have already learned to swim, or they should be learning concurrently with their sailing program.

Waterfront

Your sailing classes can be held on almost any body of water; here are some suggestions to guide you in your choice of a site.

• Do not choose a river with a strong current because if the wind dies you will have to tow your dinghies back to the base.

• You should be able to see and supervise the total sailing area.

• Other vessels should not be allowed to cross your sailing area.

• Try to avoid locating next to a public beach; it's distracting for the children and might encourage them to wander off.

• The best place is probably a cleared beach (no stumps, garbage, broken glass, etc.) or a boat dock which floats low on the water.

If you are sailing off a beach, make sure that the drop off into the water is gently graded or children will have problems getting launched and getting back to shore.

Teaching techniques

The basic principle underlying the course described in this book is *action before comprehension*. Youngsters must have as much practice on the water as possible so that they can learn for themselves what they are not able to grasp in the theoretical exercises. This is as good a method for adults as it is for youngsters.

Instructors must help students to accept the responsibility for learning and practicing each step by themselves. Each youngster should be encouraged to observe and imitate, to actively participate in games and to be curious and inventive. It is hoped that by providing an incentive in the form of graduated exercises and games each youngster will develop a sense of discipline and competition, along with the ability to make decisions about the nature of the wind and the water and the course he should follow. We are not trying to create future champions; we want youngsters to be interested enough in sailing to try to be good at it, for their own pleasure and satisfaction.

Children who are afraid of the water should be allowed to play, two to a boat, in a dinghy floating on the water, from which the sail, daggerboard and rudder have been removed. You might also show them that their life jacket will float with them in it. The presence of the rescue boat and the competence of the instructors should also reassure them.

About Chapter 1

After having read the preliminary instructions, a youngster should rig his dinghy himself. The Optimist's sprit sail rig is easy to handle and can be positioned by one person. The other boats suggested in this book are equally as easy to rig.

During this first session the youngster learns to react to many new situations; therefore the wind should be no stronger than Force 3 on the Beaufort Scale. The buoys should be placed as directed in Chapter 1, perpendicular to the direction of the wind. To make this first session easier you could tie a knot in the sheet so that the sail will not go into the broad reach position. When the dinghies are rigged you should instruct the youngsters to sit facing the sail, holding the sheet in one hand and the tiller in the other. That's all that is necessary at the moment. You should stress only two things — aim at the buoys, and keep the sail full of wind. The "wet finger" method of telling wind direction is frustrating at this time; so you could point out to them such visual signs as telltales, and wind vanes.

At this stage instructors should not issue commands to the youngsters about anything. The beam reach exercise is simple, and the students will find out themselves how their dinghy sails best. They will not handle their boat like experienced seamen, but that doesn't matter; what matters is that they experiment with the position of the sail to find the best way to keep on course.

Instructors should remain calm and interested during this first outing.

As soon as the boats have been beached, deal with any questions that the children might have. The sailing tips and follow-up exercises which come after the sessions on the water are designed to help instructors answer questions and give explanations. They provide a visual reference for technical theory. The information does not have to be learned by rote.

The time it takes for each group of children to assimilate the subject matter will vary; younger students may have to repeat the course on the water several times, as well as participating in several of the games described on page 171.

Answers to questions

The purpose of the preliminary exercises in each chapter (which should be read before setting sail) is to promote self-discipline, respect for equipment and a spirit of co-operation. Each session on the water should be easier after these exercises have been done. Reading and completing exercises such as filling in a weather report will help youngsters realize that there is a logical order to follow.

The 2nd preliminary exercise of each chapter asks the student to draw a bird's-eye view of the course he will be sailing. This exercise simplifies the explanations given by the instructors, and accustoms the youngster to map and chart work.

Answers for the first exercise in each instructional chapter
Things that must be done before setting sail
1. Read carefully the preliminary instructions for the chapter you are doing.
2. Check the weather. (If your sailing club has a small craft warning signal, know where it is located and keep your eye on it while you are sailing. Weather can change very quickly.)
3. If the weather is good enough to permit sailing, do some physical exercises (see Chapter 9).
4. Put extra clothing in a plastic bag, making sure that you have some dry clothes to put on after sailing.
5. Turn the dinghy over correctly.
6. Face your boat into the wind.
7. Rig your boat, following the steps outlined in Exercise 4.
8. If there are several of you, watch the first boat set sail.
9. Set sail following the steps outlined in Exercise 4.
10. Sail to the buoys to complete the course and play water games.

Things that must never be done

1. Do not walk on the hulls of the overturned dinghies.
2. Do not leave the beach cluttered with garbage.
3. Don't turn the boat over from the back or front, but from the side.
4. Do not get inside the dinghy to rig it.
5. Never rig your boat while underway.
6. Never take off from shore without your equipment properly in your boat.
7. Don't leave your boat unattended near the water.
8. Do not "row" with the daggerboard if you do not get away from shore successfully with the sail. This makes the boat tippy.
9. Do not leave any of your things (clothes, shoes, sail, etc.) where they might obstruct others.
10. Do not carry out your own expedition if your instructors have told you to complete a certain course around the buoys.
11. Do not play in the way of the rescue boat.
12. Do not wear boots or shoes that will fill with water if you capsize.
13. Do not set sail until your instructors are ready to help you.
14. Don't play near the water without your life jacket on.

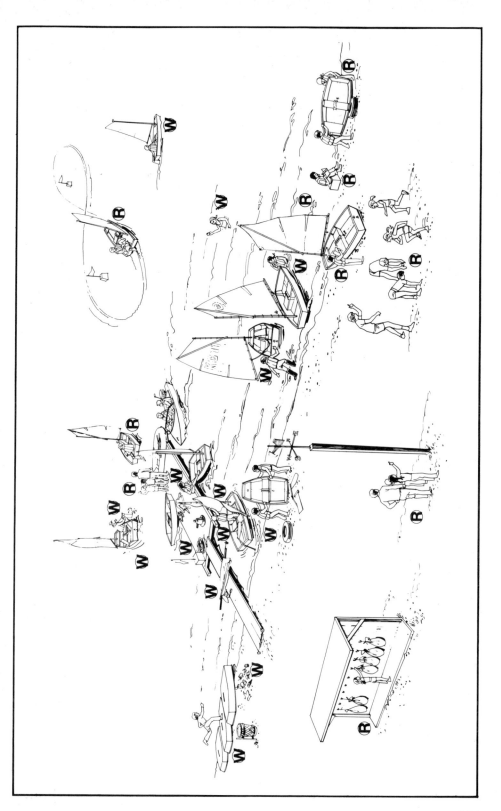

169

Sequence for rigging an Optimist

1. Inspect boat

a) flotation secure

b) bailer and lines secure

c) oars or paddles secure — with clips, retainers or lines

d) shock cord for daggerboard secure

e) all fittings secure

f) painter secure

g) all plywood surfaces sound

2. Inspect sail

a) attach sail on mast and boom

b) attach main sheet to boom

c) attach main sheet block to boom by a clove hitch and bow line

d) attach downhaul

e) fit battens

f) attach sprit

g) roll sail around mast and boom and wrap with main sheet

h) with bow to wind step mast and secure with wedges or mast clamps

i) unwrap main sheet and thread in blocks. Tie Figure 8 knot on end of sheet

j) adjust sprit for weather and downhaul

k) insert daggerboard flush with hull

3. Sailing from the beach

a) take boat to deep water and fit rudder and tiller in gudgeons. Test to see that rudder is secure.

4. Make sure children are wearing U.S. Coast Guard approved life jackets.

5. Make sure children tell you where they are going and how long they expect to be gone.

Answers to Exercise 5 –The middle boats are properly balanced.

Answer to Exercise 6 – The sheet is firmly held in one hand.

Answers to Exercise 8 – trees without leaves, trees with leaves, flag, hair, smoke, clouds (only sometimes), waves (only sometimes), weather vane.

Answers to Exercise 10 – The answers for this quiz can all be found on the pages of Chapter 1.

About Chapters 2 and 3

Following the principle "action before comprehension", youngsters should complete the courses on the water immediately after having read the preliminary instructions on pages 44 and 45 for Chapter 2 and 62 and 63 for Chapter 3.

Come back to the classroom after the water practice to answer questions, study the sailing tips and do the follow-up exercises. At this time you might introduce one of the chapters dealing with related areas — miniatures, construction, weather, etc.

Answers for these and other chapters can all be found by looking at the sailing tips in each chapter.

About Chapter 4

Read the Preliminary Instructions.

It is a good idea to give the regatta starting signal several times so that each child will get used to controlling the dinghy at the starting line.

You should not allow the youngsters to scull the rudder to get ahead.

Answers to questions in all other chapters can be worked out by looking at the text. The Beaufort reading for the picture on page 147 is Force 3.

Games

During each of the first three practice sessions on the water instructors or parents should organize water games to supplement the exercises.

Before beginning you must:
· explain carefully how each game is played
· make sure that everyone understands what signals (visual or audio) will begin and end the game
· clarify the role of the instructor in the game and explain what part the rescue boat will play.

You should emphasize the necessity of respecting the regulations governing right of way (Chapter 4) so that collisions do not occur.

Games to supplement Chapter 1

1. Water Pick-Up: Place at each buoy a pail containing different objects (balloons, balls, cups, etc.); most of these things should float. The children try to pick up the objects as they go round the buoy.

2. Duck Hunt (after the first water exercise has been repeated several times): Many floating objects are placed on the water; the youngsters manoeuvre their dinghies so they can pick them up.

3. Auto Race: Youngsters line up along the shore, a given distance away from their dinghies. When the signal is given they race to their boat, rig it as quickly as possible and set sail to complete the course.

Games to supplement Chapters 2 and 3

4. Relay Races: Children are required to keep their boat still, with the sail luffing while waiting to enter the race from the relay position. Children can use a buoy with a painter on it as a baton.

5. Water Slalom: The buoys for the course outlined in Chapter 3 (beating and running) are brought closer together so that the youngsters have to weave or slalom in and out around them. You will need extra buoys for this course.

6. Hot Potato: A soccer or beach ball is the hot potato. At the sound of the whistle the youngster who is holding the ball must throw it into another boat within 10 seconds.

7. Catch the Scarf: Each youngster attaches a scarf to the end of his boom. When the signal is given each child tries to get a scarf from another boat. Each boat must manoeuvre according to the regulations governing right of way.

8. Children aged 7 to 9 could play games which take place on the water, in a dinghy without a sail. There should be two children per boat when the sail is down. Suitable games would be:

· races
· balloon throwing
· splashing crew of other boats

9. An Expedition: Organize a short sea voyage (a day or ½ a day) to a chosen picnic spot.

10. Fishing: When there is very little wind go fishing from the boats.

11. Treasure Hunt: The prize is hidden and clues or messages are left in several places. After reading the first clue (which would be hidden on shore) the children are required to sail to where the second clue is, and perhaps come back to land for the third, etc. – lots of practice in all manoeuvres!

12. Turn Around: The children can serve as "officials" at a parents' and instructors' regatta.

13. On Rainy Days: Collect pictures of sail boats to make a scrapbook, labelling different points of sail, types of boats or wind velocities or cloud types.

Rescue

How to help a dinghy which is in trouble but has not capsized

1. Turn the dinghy so it faces into the wind if possible.

2. Move alongside the dinghy.

3. One person in the rescue boat should stand by the student's dinghy while giving him or her instructions for correcting whatever is wrong.

If the dinghy has capsized

Under usual circumstances, don't interfere. Youngsters are perfectly capable of righting a capsized dinghy by themselves. In fact they should be encouraged to practice capsizing and righting their boats at first on a calm day and later on a windy day. If for some reason a child finds it impossible to right his boat:

1. Approach the dinghy on its leeward side and turn it so that it faces into the wind if possible.

2. Have the youngster get into the rescue boat.

3. Pick up any pieces in the water (rudder, daggerboard, etc.).

4. Right the dinghy in the water if possible and pull it to safe waters where it can be bailed and rerigged.

Teaching aids you can make

· Series of plywood rudimentary model "boats" (flat bottom, moveable piece for boom) for illustrating different positions and tacks

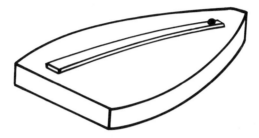

· Dock – it should be as low as possible in the water and very stable. There should be rings to tie up the dinghies.

· Floating buoy

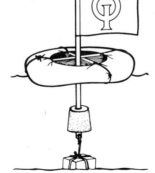

CHAPTER 14
Making your own sailing dinghy

By writing to the United States Optimist-Dinghy Association (USODA) you can obtain plans for the Optimist Sailing Dinghy and instructions for assembling it. With the help of your parents or instructors you can construct an Optimist for about $150 and 35 hours of labor.

The best way to build your Optimist dinghy is in a group for then you can buy all your supplies in bulk at a lower price. Money and time can be saved by cutting your own pieces from larger boards – and you'll find that glue, fastenings, lumber and sails are all cheaper in quantity.

Make one boat carefully at first. The instructions are clear and easy to follow. Have everyone watch and participate in the first assembly so they can learn the techniques and avoid errors when the rest of the boats are built. When you've become an expert, why not teach others to build Optimists?

The plans, building instructions, class rules, your building plaque and the US number for your sail all may be obtained by sending $15 in a money order payable to the **United States Optimist-Dinghy Association, P.O. Box 30175, Miami, Florida 33133.**

You can build as many boats from your plans as you like, but remember to register each additional boat by sending $10 to the United States Optimist-Dinghy Association for a US number and building plaque.

Materials used in the construction of a wooden Optimist
Sheets of plywood – composed of thin sheets of wood glued together. Each of the thin sheets is called a "ply"; there could be from three to five plies in a plywood sheet. The more plies the more solid will be the sheet of plywood.

Hardwood – mahogany, cedar, oak, ash

Softwood – pine, fir, spruce

Sundries – brass or stainless steel screws, bronze ring nails, marine paint, varnish. Aerolite Marine Glue and Hardener . . .

Tools

sabre saw to cut the boards
vise to hold the glued pieces
sandpaper, hammer, screwdriver, file, plane, level, drill, square, wood file, chisels, 25′ (7.26 m) tape measure.

Advantages and disadvantages of a wooden Optimist

Advantages

It can be made by anyone with a little ingenuity and manual dexterity.

It can be constructed anywhere – in a garage, basement, even outside in the summer if there is some protection from the wind.

Disadvantages

A wooden dinghy requires a lot of care (see Chapter 10) – sanding, painting, etc. because of the wearing action of sand and rocks. Repairs must be done carefully. However, if you prime coat your boat with thinned out epoxy inside and out then a wooden boat is stronger than plastic and will last just as long.

Materials used in the construction of a fibreglass Optimist
Fibreglass Resin and catalyst

Fibreglass is sold in the form of mats that can be cut with scissors. The mat can be impregnated with resin either before or after putting it in place. It is most important that it be completely covered with resin, so that there are no air bubbles. To eliminate air bubbles the surface must be smoothed carefully.

Tools
A boat "mold" is required to shape the fibreglass while it is being cut and impregnated with resin, paint roller or brush to spread and smooth the resin, gloves, sander.

Advantages and disadvantages of a fibreglass Optimist

Advantages
Requires very little care. Repairs are easily made. The hull is very durable.

Disadvantages
Special equipment and a special location are required for construction — molds, well-ventilated place, etc. although the Optimist Association of Canada can provide you with a list of builders who construct fibreglass Optimist dinghies which meet international specifications.

The Sail
Sails are best made of polyester sold under various trade names, depending on the country of origin: Dacron (U.S.A. and Canada); Terylene (Great Britain); Tergal (France).

Although a synthetic sail will not rot, it must be put away with care; you should rinse it in fresh water if it has been in salt water, because salt is like sandpaper — it roughens and wears the sail (sand has the same effect).

The sail should be hung up to dry or spread out on the grass, but never spread out on sand or concrete. Avoid excessive exposure to the sun.

Don't try to make your own sail unless you're an expert. It pays to have it made by a good sailmaker — it will last longer and your boat will sail better.

CHAPTER 15

The United States Optimist-Dinghy Association

The United States Optimist-Dinghy Association

The United States Optimist-Dinghy Association (USODA) is one of 32 national organizations which belong to the International Optimist-Dinghy Association (IODA).

As a member of IODA, USODA is the only association in the United States authorized to distribute the plans and instructions for the construction of an Optimist dinghy and to certify and register any dinghy built.

The United States Optimist-Dinghy Association is responsible for ensuring that each Optimist dinghy, whether built by an amateur or a professional builder, conforms to international standards and has the specifications of any other Optimist.

The USODA is responsible for promoting and organizing sailing in the "Optimist class"; a schedule is published by the class association listing provincial and national regattas. From among the participants in these regattas are chosen the candidates that will represent the United States in the World Championships held each year in one of the 32 member countries. So make sure you become a member of USODA so you can hear all the news about events, rules, regattas, and champions.

The USODA is interested not only in the Optimist dinghy, but in all forms of activity related to class activities. The Association is always looking for people to organize and direct these activities; if any of those listed below interest you, write to the USODA and they will tell you how you can participate.

Activities: regattas, building programs, instruction on sailing, sailing holidays, publicity, measurement clinics.

What every Optimist owner should know

1. Definition
To be an Optimist, a dinghy must meet the following conditions:

1.1 It shall have been built by any professional or amateur builder. Professional builders shall be responsible for supplying boats within the measurement rules and specifications.

1.2 It shall be built in accordance with the plans, class rules, measurement forms and diagrams.

1.3 It shall have paid a building fee to the International Yacht Racing Union (IYRU) and the International Optimist Dinghy Association (IODA) through the United States Optimist-Dinghy Association (USODA) which is the national authority of the Optimist dinghy in the United States.

1.4 On receipt of evidence that the building fee has been paid USODA shall issue a US number to the boat.

1.5 It should be measured by a measurer officially recognized by USODA

If even one of these conditions is not met the boat is not considered to be an Optimist.

There are three ways to acquire an Optimist:

- to construct one
- to buy one from a professional builder
- to buy one second hand.

2. Amateur Builder
The plans and necessary instructions are sold through USODA. You may start from scratch or you may purchase a kit. Once the boat is built, it must have a building fee receipt which is like the birth certificate of this dinghy. A record of this is kept by USODA. It must also be measured by a USODA-approved measurer. Write to USODA to obtain a list of approved measurers. If your dinghy conforms to the specifications of the IYRU, USODA will give you a measurement certificate which will permit you to participate in important provincial national and international regattas as well as other activities of the Optimist class.

3. Purchase from a professional builder

Whether you are buying a wooden dinghy or one constructed of fiberglass you must:

• ask for a building fee receipt so that the boat can have a US number.

• ask for the measurement form for the dinghy you are buying; make sure it is completed and signed by an approved measurer.

• put your name and address on the measurement form and send it to the Secretary Treasurer of USODA. You will then receive a measurement certificate which will enable you to participate in provincial, national and international ragattas as well as in all other activities of the Optimist class. Your dinghy may require remeasurement before a regatta to make sure it meets all the class rules.

4. Purchase of a second-hand Optimist

To be sure that the dinghy is an Optimist ask for the building fee receipt and the measurement certificate. The seller's name should be on the certificate.

Whether you have built your own Optimist or have purchased one from a builder, you must have a measurement certificate completed and signed by an approved measurer. Add the name and address of your club or sailing school and send the certificate to USODA. USODA will send you a new measurement form in your own name, and the Optimist dinghy bulletin which contains useful information. Please be sure to notify USODA of any change in ownership.

Successors to your small boat

All provincial and national programs sponsored by the United States Optimist Dinghy Association and by the International Optimist Dinghy Association are open to anyone between the ages of 7 and 15 years. But you can sail your Optimist at any age.

In recent years many modern, medium-priced sailboats have appeared on the market, so you should have no difficulty selecting the one which will be the best successor to the Optimist. Here are a few we recommend:

Snipe
Length: 15'6'' (4.72 m)
Width: 5'   (1.52 m)
Sail area: 128 square feet
            (11.9 square metres)

Force 5
Length: 13'10'' (4.22 m)
Width: 4'10'' (1.47 m)
Sail area: 91 square feet
            (8.5 square metres)

International 420
Length: 13'6'' (4.125 m)
Width: 5'4''   (1.625 m)
Sail area: 107 square feet
            (9.90 square metres)

International 470
Length: 4.7 m
Width: 1.5 m
Sail area: 12   square metres

Laser
Length: 4.23 m
Width: 1.37 m
Sail area: 7.06 square metres

International Fireball
Length: 4.85 m
Width: 1.35 m
Sail area: 11.07 square metres

Albacore
Length: 4.5 m
Width: 1.6 m
Sail area: 11.25 square metres

Butterfly
Length: 12'   (3.66 m)
Width: 4'6'' (1.37 m)
Sail area: 75 square feet
            (7 square metres)

SHIP'S LOG

DATE	Time on the water	Weather conditions	Person responsible	Other comments

DATE	Time on the water	Weather conditions	Person responsible	Other comments

REGATTAS

DATE	Starting position	Weather conditions	Finishing rank	Person responsible

DATE	Starting position	Weather conditions	Finishing rank	Person responsible

GLOSSARY

Words that sailors use

If you haven't been around boats you will no doubt think that many words used by sailors are strange and complicated. But you will soon find that these words passed down through the centuries are very helpful. They allow you to communicate exactly what you mean quickly and precisely. Once these words become part of your vocabulary you are no longer a landlubber!

Anemometer – an instrument that gives the speed of the wind

Barometer – an instrument that tells what the weather will be

Battens – thin slats which give support to the leech of the sail

Batten pockets – pockets into which battens fit

Beam reach – you are sailing on a beam reach when you are sailing so the wind comes across the side of your boat

Beat, beating – you are on a beat or beating when you are sailing as close as possible toward the direction from which the wind is coming. This is also called sailing close hauled.

Black bands – marks on the mast and boom which indicate the maximum outer edge of the sail

Block – a pulley

Boom – a pole attached to the mast to which the lower edge of the sail is fastened

"Boom Over" – an expression used to indicate the boat is about to gybe

Bow – the front of the boat

Broad reach – you are on a broad reach when you are sailing with the wind almost pushing your boat

Buoy – a floating marker

Buoyancy – every boat must have enough material within it to keep it afloat when it is filled with water and crew

Capsize – sailors often call capsizing "dumping". This means tipping your boat over in the water

Catboat – a boat with the mast close to the bow

Centreboard – a movable board that can be raised or lowered through the bottom of the boat. The centreboard gives your boat stability and helps to prevent it from being pushed sideways in the water by the wind.

Centreboard trunk – holds the centreboard in place

Clew – the bottom back corner of sail

Close hauled – you are sailing close hauled when you are sailing as close to the direction from which the wind is coming as possible. This is also called beating, or sailing on a beat.

Cockpit – the area of a boat where crew and passengers sit

Coming about – turning the boat into the direction from which the wind is coming so the wind blows on the opposite side of the boat. The sail passes from one side of the boat to the other.

Craft – a sailor's word for a boat

Crew – the assistants to the captain of a boat

Cringle – a hole or "eye" in the sail through which lines can pass

Daggerboard – a board that goes down through the centre of the bottom of the boat. It can be adjusted to keep the boat from being pushed sideways on the water by the wind.

Daggerboard trunk – holds the daggerboard

Dinghy – a small boat sometimes rigged with a sail

Ease, easing – to redirect a boat away from the direction from which the wind is coming. This is also known as falling off or bearing off.

Easing the sheet – letting out the sheet that controls the sail. The opposite of sheeting in.

Freeboard – the distance from the waterline to the gunwale

Foot – the bottom edge of the sail

Gear – a sailor's word for sailing equipment

Gunwale (pronounced gunnel) – the upper edge of the sides of a boat

Gybing (sometimes called jibing), to gybe – turning a boat away from the wind so that the wind blows on the opposite side of the boat. The sail passes from one side of the boat to the other.

"Gybe Ho" – a sailor's expression used to indicate that the boat is about to gybe

Halyard – a line used to raise the sail

"Hard Alee" – a sailor's expression used to indicate that the boat is coming about

Head – top corner of sail

Heel, heeling – to tip a boat to one side or the other

Helm – another name for the tiller

Helmsman – the one who steers the boat

Hiking – leaning out of a boat to keep it sailing flat on the water

Hiking straps – you hook your toes under them to keep from falling out of your boat when you are hiking

Hygrometer – instrument that indicates the amount of humidity

In irons – a boat is in irons when the bow is pointed in the direction from which the wind is coming. The sail flaps like a flag.

Jib – a triangular sail at the bow of a boat

Jib sheet – the line that controls the jib sail

Keel – the lowest permanent part of a sailboat. It has the same function as a centreboard and a daggerboard.

Keel boat – a craft with a fixed keel that extends below the hull

Ketch – a two-masted boat with the small mast in front of the tiller

Lacing – the lines on some boats that hold the sail to the mast

Landlubber – what a sailor calls a person who does not go to sea

Leeward (pronounced loo-ward) – on the sheltered side of something away from the wind.

Line – a sailor's word for a rope

Luff, luffing – the shaking or flapping of a sail when it is not filled with wind. Also the forward edge of a sail.

Luff up – to steer a boat so the bow points more towards the direction from which the wind is coming. Also called heading up or pointing up.

Mainsail – the main sail of a boat. Sometimes called "the main".

Mainsheet – the line that controls the mainsail

Mast – a pole which supports a sail

Mast step – the place in the bottom of the boat where the base of the mast rests

Mast thwart – support for the mast at the level of the gunwales

Masthead – the top of the mast

Outhaul – line at the end of the boom used to put tension on the foot of the sail

Painter – a piece of line tied to the bow of a small boat

Pinching – sailing too close to the wind. The boat moves forward slowly.

Pintels and gudgeons – pintels are pins that fit in the slots in the gudgeons. Pintels and gudgeons hold the rudder in place on the transom of a boat.

Pointing – to make the boat sail closer to the direction from which the wind is coming

Port – the left side of a boat facing the bow

Psychrometer – an instrument that indicates the amount of humidity in the air

Reach – all the points of sail between sailing close hauled and running

"Ready About" – a sailor's expression used to indicate that the boat is ready to come about

Regatta – a meeting for boat races

Rigging – a general term for all lines and wires necessary to the mast and sails. Also the word for putting the mast, etc. in place to get the boat ready for sailing.

Rudder – a movable, flat board at the stern of a boat used as a means of steering. It is controlled by a tiller, or on large boats, a wheel.

Run, running – you are on a run or running when you are sailing with the wind or are being pushed by the wind

Sail – a piece of cloth or canvas hoisted on a boat's mast used to catch the wind and move the boat over the water

Sheet – a line that controls the sail

Ship's log – a set of pages or a book where a ship's activities can be recorded

Shipshape – neat, seamanlike

Shock cord – holds the daggerboard in place

Sprit – a pole attached to the mast which keeps the sail high

Starboard – the right side of a boat facing the bow

Stays – the wires on some boats that support the mast

Stern – the back of a boat

Swivel – attaches the block to the boom

Tack – the word used to describe the side of the boat which receives the wind first. For example, you are on a starboard tack when the wind blows over the starboard side of your boat.

Tacking – sailing in the direction from which the wind is coming. The wind first blows on one side of the boat then the other.

Tiller – a wooden bar used to turn the rudder

Trimming the sail – making sure that the sail is full of wind so that the boat moves as quickly as possible over the water

Transom – the piece across the back of a boat

Thermometer – an instrument that gives the air temperature

Underway – word used to describe a boat moving through the water – "The boat is underway."

Weather vane – indicates the direction of the wind

Wind – a large air current

Wind indicator – a feather or piece of cloth on the mast that tells the direction from which the wind is coming

Windward – the side of a boat closest to the wind.

Yawl – a two-masted boat. The small mast is nearer the stern than the tiller and rudder.